This Journal belongs to:_____

Who am I an
I am a food addi
To that end my job today is to
I am powerless over food anu my life wus unmanuyeu
until I came to believe that a power greater than myself
could restore me to sanity.
Today I humbly turn my will, my thinking and my actions (my whole life)
over to the care and protection of my Higher Power.
(Anonymous, North Jersey OA Intergroup)

MW00932155

Third Step Prayer
(Alcoholics Anonymous, Fourth Edition, page 63)
God, I offer myself to Thee—
to build with me and to do with me as Thou wilt.
Relieve me of the bondage of self, that I may better do Thy will.
Take away my difficulties, that victory over them
may bear witness to those I would help
of Thy Power, Thy Love, and Thy Way of life.
May I do Thy will always!

Seventh Step Prayer
(Alcoholics Anonymous, Fourth Edition, page 76)
My Creator,
I am now willing that you should have all of me, good and bad.
I pray that you now remove from me every single defect of character
which stands in the way of my usefulness to you and my fellows.
Grant me strength, as I go out from here, to do your bidding.
Amen.

The OA Promise
(Beyond Our Wildest Dreams, page 207)
I put my hand in yours...*and together we can do what we could never do alone!*
No longer is there a sense of hopelessness, no longer must we each depend upon
our own unsteady willpower. We are all together now, reaching out our hands for
power and strength greater than ours, and as we join hands, we find love and
understanding beyond our wildest dreams.

"Reviewing our recent behaviour, keeping our Higher Power in charge of our lives,
asking for guidance, and promptly admitting our errors, becomes a sane and
satisfying way of life..."
(The Twelve Steps and Twelve Traditions of Overeaters Anonymous, Second Edition, page 74)

The Twelve Steps of Overeaters Anonymous

1. We admitted we were powerless over food—that our lives had become unmanageable.

2. Came to believe that a power greater than ourselves could restore us to sanity.

3. Made a decision to turn our will and our lives over to the care of God *as we understood Him*.

4. Made a searching and fearless moral inventory of ourselves.

5. Admitted to God, to ourselves, and to another human being the exact nature of our wrongs.

6. Were entirely ready to have God remove all these defects of character.

7. Humbly asked Him to remove our shortcomings.

8. Made a list of all persons we had harmed and became willing to make amends to them all.

9. Made direct amends to such people wherever possible, except when to do so would injure them or others.

10. Continued to take personal inventory and when we were wrong, promptly admitted it.

11. Sought through prayer and meditation to improve our conscious contact with God *as we understood Him*, praying only for knowledge of His will for us and the power to carry that out.

12. Having had a spiritual awakening as the result of these Steps, we tried to carry this message to compulsive overeaters and to practice these principles in all our affairs.

The Twelve Traditions of Overeaters Anonymous

1. Our common welfare should come first; personal recovery depends upon OA unity.

2. For our group purpose there is but one ultimate authority—a loving God as He may express Himself in our group conscience. Our leaders are but trusted servants; they do not govern.

3. The only requirement for OA membership is a desire to stop eating compulsively.

4. Each group should be autonomous except in matters affecting other groups or OA as a whole.

5. Each group has but one primary purpose—to carry its message to the compulsive overeater who still suffers.

6. An OA group ought never endorse, finance, or lend the OA name to any related facility or outside enterprise, lest problems of money, property, and prestige divert us from our primary purpose.

7. Every OA group ought to be fully self-supporting, declining outside contributions.

8. Overeaters Anonymous should remain forever nonprofessional, but our service centers may employ special workers.

9. OA, as such, ought never be organized; but we may create service boards or committees directly responsible to those they serve.

10. Overeaters Anonymous has no opinion on outside issues; hence the OA name ought never be drawn into public controversy.

11. Our public relations policy is based on attraction rather than promotion; we need always maintain personal anonymity at the level of press, radio, films, television, and other public media of communication.

12. Anonymity is the spiritual foundation of all these Traditions, ever reminding us to place principles before personalities.

Permission to use the Twelve Steps and Twelve Traditions of Alcoholics Anonymous for adaptation granted by AA World Services, Inc.

The Nine Tools of Overeaters Anonymous

A Plan of Eating - A plan of eating helps us abstain from compulsive eating. This tool helps us deal with the physical aspects of our disease and achieve physical recovery.

Sponsorship - We ask a sponsor to help us through our program of recovery on all three levels, physical, emotional, and spiritual.

Meetings - Meetings give us an opportunity to identify our common problems, confirm our common solution through the Twelve Steps, and share the gifts we receive through this program. In addition to face-to-face meetings, OA offers telephone and online meetings.

Telephone - Many members call, text, or email their sponsors and other OA members daily. Telephone or electronic contact also provides an immediate outlet for those hard-to-handle highs and lows we may experience.

Writing - Putting our thoughts and feelings down on paper helps us to better understand our actions and reactions in a way that is often not revealed to us by simply thinking or talking about them.

Literature - We read OA approved books, pamphlets, and Lifeline Magazine. Reading literature daily reinforces how to live the Twelve Steps and Twelve Traditions.

Action Plan - An action plan is the process of identifying and implementing attainable actions that are necessary to support our individual abstinence. Just like our plan of eating, it may vary widely among members and may need to be adjusted to bring structure, balance, and manageability into our lives.

Anonymity - Anonymity guarantees we will place principles before personalities and assures us that only we have the right to make our membership known within our community. Anonymity at the level of press, radio, films, television and other public media of communication means that we never allow our faces or last names to be used once we identify ourselves as OA members. Within the Fellowship, anonymity means that whatever we share with another OA member will be held in respect and confidence. What we hear at meetings should remain there.

Service - Any form of service that helps reach a fellow sufferer adds to the quality of our own recovery. Members can give service by getting to meetings, putting away chairs, putting out literature, and talking to newcomers. Beyond the group level, a member can serve as intergroup representative, committee chair, region representative, or Conference delegate. As OA's responsibility pledge states, "Always to extend the hand and heart of OA to all who share my compulsion; for this, I am responsible."

The Spiritual Principles of the Twelve Steps

Step One – Honesty

Step Two – Hope

Step Three – Faith

Step Four – Courage

Step Five – Integrity

Step Six – Willingness

Step Seven – Humility

Step Eight – Self-Discipline

Step Nine – Love

Step Ten – Perseverance

Step Eleven – Spiritual Awareness

Step Twelve - Service

The Spiritual Principles of the Twelve Traditions

Tradition One – Unity

Tradition Two – Trust

Tradition Three – Identity

Tradition Four – Autonomy

Tradition Five – Purpose

Tradition Six – Solidarity

Tradition Seven – Responsibility

Tradition Eight – Fellowship

Tradition Nine – Structure

Tradition Ten – Neutrality

Tradition Eleven – Anonymity

Tradition Twelve – Spirituality

Morning Review:
(Review prayers from first page).

Plan of Eating: *Today, extra food is not an option.*

Water: ☐☐☐☐☐☐☐☐

Breakfast:_____
_____
_____

Lunch: _____
_____
_____

Dinner: _____
_____
_____

Snack:_____
_____
_____

Gratitudes: (*A grateful heart doesn't need to eat compulsively*)
Today, I thank God for:

_____
_____
_____
_____
_____
_____

Something I like about myself:

_____
_____
_____
_____

Something to keep in mind today:

_____
_____
_____
_____

Daily Writing: Source: _____ Pages: _____

_____
_____
_____
_____
_____
_____
_____
_____
_____
_____
_____
_____
_____
_____

Su   M   Tu   W   Th   F   Sat   Date: _____ Day #:_____

Evening Review: *(or anytime the need arises)*

Today was I:

   Resentful?   _____

   _____

   Selfish?   _____

   _____

   Dishonest?   _____

   _____

   Jealous?   _____

   _____

   Fearful: (Of losing something? Of not getting what I want? Of being found out?)

   _____

   _____

   *Restless, irritable or discontented?*_____

   _____

Was I kind and loving towards all? _____

_____

_____

*Do I owe an apology?*_____

_____

_____

What did I do for others? _____

_____

_____

*What could I have done better?*_____

_____

_____

*What did I do well?*_____

_____

_____

Freedom from Bondage: Refer to the "Self Will * God's Will" chart and the "Freedom from Bondage" reading on the last pages of this journal.

God grant me freedom from _____ *and replace it with* _____
God grant me freedom from _____ *and replace it with* _____
God grant me freedom from _____ *and replace it with* _____
God grant me freedom from _____ *and replace it with* _____

*God, I pray for the health, prosperity, happiness and well-being of*_____
All the things I pray for myself, I pray also for _____

Review Eleventh Step Prayer on the last page of journal.

Morning Review:

(Review prayers from first page).

Plan of Eating: *Today, extra food is not an option.*

Water: ☐☐☐☐☐☐☐

Breakfast:_____

_____

_____

Lunch: _____

_____

_____

Dinner: _____

_____

_____

Snack:_____

_____

_____

Gratitudes: *(A grateful heart doesn't need to eat compulsively) Today, I thank God for:*

_____

_____

_____

_____

_____

_____

Something I like about myself:

_____

_____

_____

_____

Something to keep in mind today:

_____

_____

_____

_____

Daily Writing: Source: _____ Pages: _____

_____

_____

_____

_____

_____

_____

_____

_____

_____

_____

_____

_____

_____

_____

Su   M   Tu   W   Th   F   Sat   *Date:* _____ *Day #:*_____

Evening Review: *(or anytime the need arises)*

Today was I:

   Resentful?   _____

                      _____

   Selfish?   _____

                      _____

   Dishonest?   _____

                      _____

   Jealous?   _____

                      _____

   Fearful: (Of losing something? Of not getting what I want? Of being found out?)

                      _____

                      _____

   *Restless, irritable or discontented?*_____

                      _____

Was I kind and loving towards all? _____

_____

_____

*Do I owe an apology?*_____

_____

_____

What did I do for others? _____

_____

_____

*What could I have done better?*_____

_____

_____

*What did I do well?*_____

_____

_____

Freedom from Bondage: Refer to the "Self Will * God's Will" chart and the "Freedom from Bondage" reading on the last pages of this journal.

God grant me freedom from _____ *and replace it with* _____
God grant me freedom from _____ *and replace it with* _____
God grant me freedom from _____ *and replace it with* _____
God grant me freedom from _____ *and replace it with* _____

*God, I pray for the health, prosperity, happiness and well-being of*_____
All the things I pray for myself, I pray also for _____

Review Eleventh Step Prayer on the last page of journal.

Morning Review:

(Review prayers from first page).

Plan of Eating: *Today, extra food is not an option.*

Water: ☐☐☐☐☐☐☐☐

Breakfast:_____
_____
_____

Lunch: _____
_____
_____

Dinner: _____
_____
_____

Snack:_____
_____
_____

Gratitudes: *(A grateful heart doesn't need to eat compulsively)*
Today, I thank God for:
_____
_____
_____
_____
_____
_____

Something I like about myself:
_____
_____
_____
_____
_____

Something to keep in mind today:
_____
_____
_____
_____

Daily Writing: Source: _____ Pages: _____
_____
_____
_____
_____
_____
_____
_____
_____
_____
_____
_____
_____
_____
_____
_____

Evening Review: *(or anytime the need arises)*

Today was I:

   Resentful? _____

_____

   Selfish? _____

_____

   Dishonest? _____

_____

   Jealous? _____

_____

   Fearful: (Of losing something? Of not getting what I want? Of being found out?)

_____

_____

   *Restless, irritable or discontented?*_____

_____

Was I kind and loving towards all? _____

_____

_____

*Do I owe an apology?*_____

_____

_____

What did I do for others? _____

_____

_____

*What could I have done better?*_____

_____

_____

*What did I do well?*_____

_____

_____

Freedom from Bondage: Refer to the "Self Will * God's Will" chart and the "Freedom from Bondage" reading on the last pages of this journal.

God grant me freedom from _____ *and replace it with* _____
God grant me freedom from _____ *and replace it with* _____
God grant me freedom from _____ *and replace it with* _____
God grant me freedom from _____ *and replace it with* _____

*God, I pray for the health, prosperity, happiness and well-being of*_____
All the things I pray for myself, I pray also for _____

Review Eleventh Step Prayer on the last page of journal.

Morning Review:

(Review prayers from first page).

Plan of Eating: *Today, extra food is not an option.*

Water: ☐☐☐☐☐☐☐

Breakfast:_____
_____
_____

Lunch: _____
_____
_____

Dinner: _____
_____
_____

Snack:_____
_____
_____

Gratitudes: (*A grateful heart doesn't need to eat compulsively*) *Today, I thank God for*:

_____
_____
_____
_____
_____
_____

Something I like about myself:

_____
_____
_____
_____
_____

Something to keep in mind today:

_____
_____
_____
_____
_____

Daily Writing: Source: _____ Pages: _____

_____
_____
_____
_____
_____
_____
_____
_____
_____
_____
_____
_____
_____
_____

Su M Tu W Th F Sat   Date: _____ Day #:_____

Evening Review: *(or anytime the need arises)*

Today was I:

    Resentful? _____

    _____

    Selfish? _____

    _____

    Dishonest? _____

    _____

    Jealous? _____

    _____

    Fearful: (Of losing something? Of not getting what I want? Of being found out?)

    _____

    _____

    *Restless, irritable or discontented?*_____

    _____

Was I kind and loving towards all? _____

_____

_____

*Do I owe an apology?*_____

_____

_____

What did I do for others? _____

_____

_____

*What could I have done better?*_____

_____

_____

*What did I do well?*_____

_____

_____

Freedom from Bondage: Refer to the "Self Will * God's Will" chart and the "Freedom from Bondage" reading on the last pages of this journal.

God grant me freedom from _____ *and replace it with* _____
God grant me freedom from _____ *and replace it with* _____
God grant me freedom from _____ *and replace it with* _____
God grant me freedom from _____ *and replace it with* _____

*God, I pray for the health, prosperity, happiness and well-being of*_____
All the things I pray for myself, I pray also for _____

Review Eleventh Step Prayer on the last page of journal.

Morning Review:
(Review prayers from first page).

Plan of Eating: *Today, extra food is not an option.*

Water: ☐☐☐☐☐☐☐

Breakfast:_____
_____
_____

Lunch: _____
_____
_____

Dinner: _____
_____
_____

Snack:_____
_____
_____

Gratitudes: *(A grateful heart doesn't need to eat compulsively)* Today, I thank God for:
_____
_____
_____
_____
_____
_____

Something I like about myself:
_____
_____
_____
_____

Something to keep in mind today:
_____
_____
_____
_____

Daily Writing: Source: _____ Pages: _____

_____
_____
_____
_____
_____
_____
_____
_____
_____
_____
_____
_____
_____
_____

Su   M   Tu   W   Th   F   Sat   Date: _____ Day #:_____

Evening Review: *(or anytime the need arises)*

Today was I:

　　Resentful? _____

　　_____

　　Selfish? _____

　　_____

　　Dishonest? _____

　　_____

　　Jealous? _____

　　_____

　　Fearful: (Of losing something? Of not getting what I want? Of being found out?)

　　_____

　　_____

　　*Restless, irritable or discontented?*_____

　　_____

Was I kind and loving towards all? _____

_____

_____

*Do I owe an apology?*_____

_____

_____

What did I do for others? _____

_____

_____

*What could I have done better?*_____

_____

_____

*What did I do well?*_____

_____

_____

Freedom from Bondage: Refer to the "Self Will * God's Will" chart and the "Freedom from Bondage" reading on the last pages of this journal.

God grant me freedom from _____ *and replace it with* _____
God grant me freedom from _____ *and replace it with* _____
God grant me freedom from _____ *and replace it with* _____
God grant me freedom from _____ *and replace it with* _____

*God, I pray for the health, prosperity, happiness and well-being of*_____
All the things I pray for myself, I pray also for _____

Review Eleventh Step Prayer on the last page of journal.

Morning Review:

(*Review prayers from first page*).

Plan of Eating: *Today, extra food is not an option.*

Water: ☐☐☐☐☐☐☐

Breakfast:_____

_____

_____

Lunch: _____

_____

_____

Dinner: _____

_____

_____

Snack:_____

_____

_____

Gratitudes: (*A grateful heart doesn't need to eat compulsively*) *Today, I thank God for:*

_____

_____

_____

_____

_____

_____

Something I like about myself:

_____

_____

_____

_____

_____

Something to keep in mind today:

_____

_____

_____

_____

_____

Daily Writing: Source: _____ Pages: _____

_____

_____

_____

_____

_____

_____

_____

_____

_____

_____

_____

_____

_____

_____

Su   M   Tu   W   Th   F   Sat   *Date:* _____ *Day #:* _____

Evening Review: *(or anytime the need arises)*

Today was I:

  Resentful? _____
  _____

  Selfish? _____
  _____

  Dishonest? _____
  _____

  Jealous? _____
  _____

  Fearful: (Of losing something? Of not getting what I want? Of being found out?)
  _____
  _____

  Restless, irritable or discontented? _____
  _____

Was I kind and loving towards all? _____
_____
_____

Do I owe an apology? _____
_____
_____

What did I do for others? _____
_____
_____

What could I have done better? _____
_____
_____

What did I do well? _____
_____
_____

Freedom from Bondage: Refer to the "Self Will * God's Will" chart and the "Freedom from Bondage" reading on the last pages of this journal.

God grant me freedom from _____ *and replace it with* _____
God grant me freedom from _____ *and replace it with* _____
God grant me freedom from _____ *and replace it with* _____
God grant me freedom from _____ *and replace it with* _____

God, I pray for the health, prosperity, happiness and well-being of _____
All the things I pray for myself, I pray also for _____

Review Eleventh Step Prayer on the last page of journal.

Morning Review:
(Review prayers from first page).

Plan of Eating: *Today, extra food is not an option.*

Water: ☐☐☐☐☐☐☐

Breakfast:_____
_____
_____

Lunch: _____
_____
_____

Dinner: _____
_____
_____

Snack:_____
_____
_____

Gratitudes: (*A grateful heart doesn't need to eat compulsively*) *Today, I thank God for:*

_____
_____
_____
_____
_____
_____

Something I like about myself:

_____
_____
_____
_____
_____

Something to keep in mind today:

_____
_____
_____
_____

Daily Writing: Source: _____ Pages: _____

_____
_____
_____
_____
_____
_____
_____
_____
_____
_____
_____
_____
_____
_____
_____

Su   M   Tu   W   Th   F   Sat   Date: _____ Day #:_____

Evening Review: (or anytime the need arises)

Today was I:

Resentful? _____
_____

Selfish? _____
_____

Dishonest? _____
_____

Jealous? _____
_____

Fearful: (Of losing something? Of not getting what I want? Of being found out?)
_____
_____

Restless, irritable or discontented?_____
_____

Was I kind and loving towards all? _____
_____
_____

Do I owe an apology?_____
_____
_____

What did I do for others? _____
_____
_____

What could I have done better?_____
_____
_____

What did I do well?_____
_____
_____

Freedom from Bondage: Refer to the "Self Will * God's Will" chart and the "Freedom from Bondage" reading on the last pages of this journal.

God grant me freedom from   _____ and replace it with _____
God grant me freedom from   _____ and replace it with _____
God grant me freedom from   _____ and replace it with _____
God grant me freedom from   _____ and replace it with _____

God, I pray for the health, prosperity, happiness and well-being of_____
All the things I pray for myself, I pray also for _____

Review Eleventh Step Prayer on the last page of journal.

Morning Review:

(Review prayers from first page).

Plan of Eating: *Today, extra food is not an option.*

Water: ☐☐☐☐☐☐☐

Breakfast:_____

_____

_____

Lunch: _____

_____

_____

Dinner: _____

_____

_____

Snack:_____

_____

_____

Gratitudes: *(A grateful heart doesn't need to eat compulsively)*
Today, I thank God for:

_____

_____

_____

_____

_____

_____

Something I like about myself:

_____

_____

_____

_____

Something to keep in mind today:

_____

_____

_____

_____

Daily Writing: Source: _____ Pages: _____

_____

_____

_____

_____

_____

_____

_____

_____

_____

_____

_____

_____

_____

_____

Su   M   Tu   W   Th   F   Sat   Date: _____   Day #:_____

Evening Review: *(or anytime the need arises)*

Today was I:

Resentful? _____

_____

Selfish? _____

_____

Dishonest? _____

_____

Jealous? _____

_____

Fearful: (Of losing something? Of not getting what I want? Of being found out?)

_____

_____

Restless, irritable or discontented?_____

_____

Was I kind and loving towards all? _____

_____

_____

*Do I owe an apology?*_____

_____

_____

What did I do for others? _____

_____

_____

*What could I have done better?*_____

_____

_____

*What did I do well?*_____

_____

_____

Freedom from Bondage: Refer to the "Self Will * God's Will" chart and the "Freedom from Bondage" reading on the last pages of this journal.

God grant me freedom from _____ *and replace it with* _____
God grant me freedom from _____ *and replace it with* _____
God grant me freedom from _____ *and replace it with* _____
God grant me freedom from _____ *and replace it with* _____

*God, I pray for the health, prosperity, happiness and well-being of*_____
All the things I pray for myself, I pray also for _____

Review Eleventh Step Prayer on the last page of journal.

Morning Review:

(Review prayers from first page).

Plan of Eating: *Today, extra food is not an option.*

Water: ☐☐☐☐☐☐☐☐

Breakfast:_____

_____

_____

Lunch: _____

_____

_____

Dinner: _____

_____

_____

Snack:_____

_____

_____

Gratitudes: *(A grateful heart doesn't need to eat compulsively)*
Today, I thank God for:

_____

_____

_____

_____

_____

_____

Something I like about myself:

_____

_____

_____

_____

_____

Something to keep in mind today:

_____

_____

_____

_____

_____

Daily Writing: Source: _____ Pages: _____

_____

_____

_____

_____

_____

_____

_____

_____

_____

_____

_____

_____

_____

_____

_____

Su   M   Tu   W   Th   F   Sat   Date: _____   Day #:_____

Evening Review: *(or anytime the need arises)*

Today was I:

   Resentful?   _____

                                  _____

   Selfish?   _____

                                  _____

   Dishonest?   _____

                                  _____

   Jealous?   _____

   Fearful: (Of losing something? Of not getting what I want? Of being found out?)

                                  _____

                                  _____

   *Restless, irritable or discontented?*_____

                                  _____

Was I kind and loving towards all? _____

_____

*Do I owe an apology?*_____

_____

What did I do for others? _____

_____

*What could I have done better?*_____

_____

*What did I do well?*_____

_____

Freedom from Bondage: Refer to the "Self Will * God's Will" chart and the "Freedom from Bondage" reading on the last pages of this journal.

God grant me freedom from _____ *and replace it with* _____
God grant me freedom from _____ *and replace it with* _____
God grant me freedom from _____ *and replace it with* _____
God grant me freedom from _____ *and replace it with* _____

*God, I pray for the health, prosperity, happiness and well-being of*_____
All the things I pray for myself, I pray also for _____

Review Eleventh Step Prayer on the last page of journal.

Morning Review:
(*Review prayers from first page*).

Plan of Eating: *Today, extra food is not an option.*

Water: ☐☐☐☐☐☐☐

Breakfast:_____
_____
_____

Lunch: _____
_____
_____

Dinner: _____
_____
_____

Snack:_____
_____
_____

Gratitudes: (*A grateful heart doesn't need to eat compulsively*)
Today, I thank God for:

_____
_____
_____
_____
_____
_____

Something I like about myself:

_____
_____
_____
_____
_____

Something to keep in mind today:

_____
_____
_____
_____
_____

Daily Writing: Source: _____ Pages: _____

_____
_____
_____
_____
_____
_____
_____
_____
_____
_____
_____
_____
_____
_____
_____

Su   M   Tu   W   Th   F   Sat   Date: _____ Day #:_____

Evening Review: *(or anytime the need arises)*

Today was I:

   Resentful? _____

_____

   Selfish? _____

_____

   Dishonest? _____

_____

   Jealous? _____

_____

   Fearful: (Of losing something? Of not getting what I want? Of being found out?)

_____

_____

   *Restless, irritable or discontented?*_____

_____

Was I kind and loving towards all? _____

_____

_____

Do I owe an apology? _____

_____

_____

What did I do for others? _____

_____

_____

*What could I have done better?*_____

_____

_____

*What did I do well?*_____

_____

_____

Freedom from Bondage: Refer to the "Self Will * God's Will" chart and the "Freedom from Bondage" reading on the last pages of this journal.

God grant me freedom from _____ *and replace it with* _____
God grant me freedom from _____ *and replace it with* _____
God grant me freedom from _____ *and replace it with* _____
God grant me freedom from _____ *and replace it with* _____

*God, I pray for the health, prosperity, happiness and well-being of*_____
All the things I pray for myself, I pray also for _____

Review Eleventh Step Prayer on the last page of journal.

Morning Review:
(*Review prayers from first page*).

Plan of Eating: *Today, extra food is not an option.*

Water: ☐☐☐☐☐☐☐

Breakfast:_____

_____

_____

Lunch: _____

_____

_____

Dinner: _____

_____

_____

Snack:_____

_____

_____

Gratitudes: (*A grateful heart doesn't need to eat compulsively*) *Today, I thank God for*:

_____

_____

_____

_____

_____

_____

Something I like about myself:

_____

_____

_____

_____

Something to keep in mind today:

_____

_____

_____

_____

_____

Daily Writing: Source: _____ Pages: _____

_____

_____

_____

_____

_____

_____

_____

_____

_____

_____

_____

_____

_____

_____

_____

Su   M   Tu   W   Th   F   Sat   Date: _____ Day #:_____

Evening Review: *(or anytime the need arises)*

Today was I:

Resentful?   _____

_____

Selfish?   _____

_____

Dishonest?   _____

_____

Jealous?   _____

_____

Fearful: (Of losing something? Of not getting what I want? Of being found out?)

_____

_____

Restless, irritable or discontented?_____

_____

Was I kind and loving towards all? _____

_____

_____

Do I owe an apology? _____

_____

_____

What did I do for others? _____

_____

_____

*What could I have done better?*_____

_____

_____

*What did I do well?*_____

_____

_____

Freedom from Bondage: Refer to the "Self Will * God's Will" chart and the "Freedom from Bondage" reading on the last pages of this journal.

God grant me freedom from _____ *and replace it with* _____
God grant me freedom from _____ *and replace it with* _____
God grant me freedom from _____ *and replace it with* _____
God grant me freedom from _____ *and replace it with* _____

*God, I pray for the health, prosperity, happiness and well-being of*_____
All the things I pray for myself, I pray also for _____

Review Eleventh Step Prayer on the last page of journal.

Morning Review:

(Review prayers from first page).

Plan of Eating: *Today, extra food is not an option.*

Water: ☐☐☐☐☐☐☐

Breakfast:_____

_____

_____

Lunch: _____

_____

_____

Dinner: _____

_____

_____

Snack:_____

_____

_____

Gratitudes: *(A grateful heart doesn't need to eat compulsively)* Today, I thank God for:

_____

_____

_____

_____

_____

_____

Something I like about myself:

_____

_____

_____

_____

Something to keep in mind today:

_____

_____

_____

_____

Daily Writing: Source: _____ Pages: _____

_____

_____

_____

_____

_____

_____

_____

_____

_____

_____

_____

_____

_____

_____

Su   M   Tu   W   Th   F   Sat   Date: _____ Day #:_____

Evening Review: *(or anytime the need arises)*

Today was I:

   Resentful?   _____

                       _____

   Selfish?   _____

                       _____

   Dishonest?   _____

                       _____

   Jealous?   _____

                       _____

   Fearful: (Of losing something? Of not getting what I want? Of being found out?)

                       _____

                       _____

   Restless, irritable or discontented?_____

                       _____

Was I kind and loving towards all? _____

_____

_____

*Do I owe an apology?*_____

_____

_____

What did I do for others? _____

_____

_____

*What could I have done better?*_____

_____

_____

*What did I do well?*_____

_____

_____

Freedom from Bondage: Refer to the "Self Will * God's Will" chart and the "Freedom from Bondage" reading on the last pages of this journal.

God grant me freedom from _____ *and replace it with* _____
God grant me freedom from _____ *and replace it with* _____
God grant me freedom from _____ *and replace it with* _____
God grant me freedom from _____ *and replace it with* _____

*God, I pray for the health, prosperity, happiness and well-being of*_____
All the things I pray for myself, I pray also for _____

Review Eleventh Step Prayer on the last page of journal.

Morning Review:

(Review prayers from first page).

Plan of Eating: *Today, extra food is not an option.*

Water: ☐☐☐☐☐☐☐

Breakfast:_____

_____

_____

Lunch: _____

_____

_____

Dinner: _____

_____

_____

Snack:_____

_____

_____

Gratitudes: (*A grateful heart doesn't need to eat compulsively*) *Today, I thank God for*:

_____

_____

_____

_____

_____

Something I like about myself:

_____

_____

_____

_____

_____

Something to keep in mind today:

_____

_____

_____

_____

_____

Daily Writing: Source: _____ Pages: _____

_____

_____

_____

_____

_____

_____

_____

_____

_____

_____

_____

_____

_____

_____

Su   M   Tu   W   Th   F   Sat   Date: _____   Day #:_____

Evening Review: *(or anytime the need arises)*

Today was I:

   Resentful? _____

                    _____

   Selfish? _____

                    _____

   Dishonest? _____

                    _____

   Jealous? _____

                    _____

   Fearful: (Of losing something? Of not getting what I want? Of being found out?)

                    _____

                    _____

   *Restless, irritable or discontented?*_____

                    _____

Was I kind and loving towards all? _____

_____

*Do I owe an apology?*_____

_____

What did I do for others? _____

_____

*What could I have done better?*_____

_____

*What did I do well?*_____

_____

_____

Freedom from Bondage: Refer to the "Self Will * God's Will" chart and the "Freedom from Bondage" reading on the last pages of this journal.

God grant me freedom from _____ *and replace it with* _____
God grant me freedom from _____ *and replace it with* _____
God grant me freedom from _____ *and replace it with* _____
God grant me freedom from _____ *and replace it with* _____

*God, I pray for the health, prosperity, happiness and well-being of*_____
All the things I pray for myself, I pray also for _____

Review Eleventh Step Prayer on the last page of journal.

Morning Review:

(Review prayers from first page).

Plan of Eating: *Today, extra food is not an option.*

Water: ☐☐☐☐☐☐☐

Breakfast:_____

_____

_____

Lunch: _____

_____

_____

Dinner: _____

_____

_____

Snack:_____

_____

_____

Gratitudes: *(A grateful heart doesn't need to eat compulsively)*

Today, I thank God for:

_____

_____

_____

_____

_____

_____

Something I like about myself:

_____

_____

_____

_____

Something to keep in mind today:

_____

_____

_____

_____

_____

Daily Writing: Source: _____ Pages: _____

_____

_____

_____

_____

_____

_____

_____

_____

_____

_____

_____

_____

_____

_____

Su   M   Tu   W   Th   F   Sat   Date: _____ Day #:_____

Evening Review: *(or anytime the need arises)*

Today was I:

    Resentful?   _____

_____

    Selfish?   _____

_____

    Dishonest?   _____

_____

    Jealous?   _____

_____

    Fearful: (Of losing something? Of not getting what I want? Of being found out?)

_____

_____

    *Restless, irritable or discontented?*_____

_____

Was I kind and loving towards all? _____

_____

_____

*Do I owe an apology?*_____

_____

What did I do for others? _____

_____

_____

*What could I have done better?*_____

_____

_____

*What did I do well?*_____

_____

_____

Freedom from Bondage: Refer to the "Self Will * God's Will" chart and the "Freedom from Bondage" reading on the last pages of this journal.

God grant me freedom from _____ *and replace it with* _____
God grant me freedom from _____ *and replace it with* _____
God grant me freedom from _____ *and replace it with* _____
God grant me freedom from _____ *and replace it with* _____

*God, I pray for the health, prosperity, happiness and well-being of*_____
All the things I pray for myself, I pray also for _____

Review Eleventh Step Prayer on the last page of journal.

Morning Review:

(Review prayers from first page).

Plan of Eating: *Today, extra food is not an option.*

Water: ☐☐☐☐☐☐☐

Breakfast:_____

_____

_____

Lunch: _____

_____

_____

Dinner: _____

_____

_____

Snack:_____

_____

_____

Gratitudes: *(A grateful heart doesn't need to eat compulsively)* *Today, I thank God for:*

_____

_____

_____

_____

_____

_____

Something I like about myself:

_____

_____

_____

_____

Something to keep in mind today:

_____

_____

_____

_____

Daily Writing: Source: _____ Pages: _____

_____

_____

_____

_____

_____

_____

_____

_____

_____

_____

_____

_____

_____

_____

Su   M   Tu   W   Th   F   Sat   Date: _____ Day #:_____

Evening Review: *(or anytime the need arises)*

Today was I:

   Resentful?   _____

                _____

   Selfish?   _____

                _____

   Dishonest?   _____

                _____

   Jealous?   _____

   Fearful: (Of losing something? Of not getting what I want? Of being found out?)

                _____

                _____

   Restless, irritable or discontented?_____

                _____

Was I kind and loving towards all? _____

_____

_____

*Do I owe an apology?*_____

_____

What did I do for others? _____

_____

*What could I have done better?*_____

_____

_____

*What did I do well?*_____

_____

_____

Freedom from Bondage: Refer to the "Self Will * God's Will" chart and the "Freedom from Bondage" reading on the last pages of this journal.

God grant me freedom from _____ *and replace it with* _____
God grant me freedom from _____ *and replace it with* _____
God grant me freedom from _____ *and replace it with* _____
God grant me freedom from _____ *and replace it with* _____

*God, I pray for the health, prosperity, happiness and well-being of*_____
All the things I pray for myself, I pray also for _____

Review Eleventh Step Prayer on the last page of journal.

Morning Review:
(Review prayers from first page).

Plan of Eating: *Today, extra food is not an option.*

Water: ☐☐☐☐☐☐☐

Breakfast:_____
_____
_____

Lunch: _____
_____
_____

Dinner: _____
_____
_____

Snack:_____
_____
_____

Gratitudes: *(A grateful heart doesn't need to eat compulsively)* Today, I thank God for:

_____
_____
_____
_____
_____
_____

Something I like about myself:

_____
_____
_____
_____
_____

Something to keep in mind today:

_____
_____
_____
_____
_____

Daily Writing: Source: _____ Pages: _____

_____
_____
_____
_____
_____
_____
_____
_____
_____
_____
_____
_____
_____
_____

Su   M   Tu   W   Th   F   Sat   *Date:* _____ *Day #:*_____

Evening Review: *(or anytime the need arises)*

Today was I:

   Resentful? _____

   _____

   Selfish? _____

   _____

   Dishonest? _____

   _____

   Jealous? _____

   _____

   Fearful: (Of losing something? Of not getting what I want? Of being found out?)

   _____

   _____

   *Restless, irritable or discontented?*_____

   _____

Was I kind and loving towards all? _____

_____

_____

*Do I owe an apology?*_____

_____

_____

What did I do for others? _____

_____

_____

*What could I have done better?*_____

_____

_____

*What did I do well?*_____

_____

_____

Freedom from Bondage: Refer to the "Self Will * God's Will" chart and the "Freedom from Bondage" reading on the last pages of this journal.

God grant me freedom from _____ *and replace it with* _____
God grant me freedom from _____ *and replace it with* _____
God grant me freedom from _____ *and replace it with* _____
God grant me freedom from _____ *and replace it with* _____

*God, I pray for the health, prosperity, happiness and well-being of*_____
All the things I pray for myself, I pray also for _____

Review Eleventh Step Prayer on the last page of journal.

Morning Review:

(Review prayers from first page).

Plan of Eating: *Today, extra food is not an option.*

Water: ☐☐☐☐☐☐☐

Breakfast:_____
_____
_____

Lunch: _____
_____
_____

Dinner: _____
_____
_____

Snack:_____
_____
_____

Gratitudes: *(A grateful heart doesn't need to eat compulsively)*

Today, I thank God for:
_____
_____
_____
_____
_____
_____

Something I like about myself:
_____
_____
_____
_____
_____

Something to keep in mind today:
_____
_____
_____
_____
_____

Daily Writing: Source: _____ Pages: _____

_____
_____
_____
_____
_____
_____
_____
_____
_____
_____
_____
_____
_____
_____

Su   M   Tu   W   Th   F   Sat   *Date:* _____ *Day #:*_____

Evening Review: *(or anytime the need arises)*

Today was I:

   Resentful? _____

_____

   Selfish? _____

_____

   Dishonest? _____

_____

   Jealous? _____

_____

   Fearful: (Of losing something? Of not getting what I want? Of being found out?)

_____

_____

   *Restless, irritable or discontented?*_____

_____

Was I kind and loving towards all? _____

_____

_____

*Do I owe an apology?*_____

_____

_____

What did I do for others? _____

_____

_____

*What could I have done better?*_____

_____

_____

*What did I do well?*_____

_____

_____

Freedom from Bondage: Refer to the "Self Will * God's Will" chart and the "Freedom from Bondage" reading on the last pages of this journal.

God grant me freedom from _____ *and replace it with* _____
God grant me freedom from _____ *and replace it with* _____
God grant me freedom from _____ *and replace it with* _____
God grant me freedom from _____ *and replace it with* _____

*God, I pray for the health, prosperity, happiness and well-being of*_____
All the things I pray for myself, I pray also for _____

Review Eleventh Step Prayer on the last page of journal.

Morning Review:

(*Review prayers from first page*).

Plan of Eating: *Today, extra food is not an option.*

Water: ☐☐☐☐☐☐☐☐

Breakfast:_____

_____

_____

Lunch: _____

_____

_____

Dinner: _____

_____

_____

Snack:_____

_____

_____

Gratitudes: (*A grateful heart doesn't need to eat compulsively*) *Today, I thank God for:*

_____

_____

_____

_____

_____

_____

Something I like about myself:

_____

_____

_____

_____

Something to keep in mind today:

_____

_____

_____

_____

Daily Writing: Source: _____ Pages: _____

_____

_____

_____

_____

_____

_____

_____

_____

_____

_____

_____

_____

_____

_____

Su M Tu W Th F Sat   Date: _____ Day #:_____

Evening Review: *(or anytime the need arises)*

Today was I:

   Resentful?   _____

                     _____

   Selfish?   _____

   Dishonest?   _____

   Jealous?   _____

   Fearful: (Of losing something? Of not getting what I want? Of being found out?)

                     _____

   Restless, irritable or discontented?_____

                     _____

Was I kind and loving towards all? _____

_____

Do I owe an apology?_____

_____

What did I do for others? _____

_____

What could I have done better?_____

_____

What did I do well?_____

_____

_____

Freedom from Bondage: Refer to the "Self Will * God's Will" chart and the "Freedom from Bondage" reading on the last pages of this journal.

God grant me freedom from   _____ *and replace it with* _____
God grant me freedom from   _____ *and replace it with* _____
God grant me freedom from   _____ *and replace it with* _____
God grant me freedom from   _____ *and replace it with* _____

God, I pray for the health, prosperity, happiness and well-being of_____
All the things I pray for myself, I pray also for _____

Review Eleventh Step Prayer on the last page of journal.

Morning Review:
(*Review prayers from first page*).

Plan of Eating: *Today, extra food is not an option.*

Water: ☐☐☐☐☐☐☐

Breakfast:_____
_____
_____

Lunch: _____
_____
_____

Dinner: _____
_____
_____

Snack:_____
_____
_____

Gratitudes: (*A grateful heart doesn't need to eat compulsively*)
Today, I thank God for:

_____
_____
_____
_____
_____
_____

Something I like about myself:

_____
_____
_____
_____
_____

Something to keep in mind today:

_____
_____
_____
_____
_____

Daily Writing: Source: _____ Pages: _____

_____
_____
_____
_____
_____
_____
_____
_____
_____
_____
_____
_____
_____
_____
_____
_____

Su   M   Tu   W   Th   F   Sat   Date: _____ Day #:_____

Evening Review: *(or anytime the need arises)*

Today was I:

Resentful?   _____

_____

Selfish?   _____

_____

Dishonest?   _____

_____

Jealous?   _____

_____

Fearful: (Of losing something? Of not getting what I want? Of being found out?)

_____

_____

Restless, irritable or discontented?_____

_____

Was I kind and loving towards all? _____

_____

Do I owe an apology?_____

_____

What did I do for others? _____

_____

What could I have done better?_____

_____

What did I do well?_____

_____

_____

Freedom from Bondage: Refer to the "Self Will * God's Will" chart and the "Freedom from Bondage" reading on the last pages of this journal.

God grant me freedom from   _____ and replace it with _____

God grant me freedom from   _____ and replace it with _____

God grant me freedom from   _____ and replace it with _____

God grant me freedom from   _____ and replace it with _____

God, I pray for the health, prosperity, happiness and well-being of_____

All the things I pray for myself, I pray also for _____

Review Eleventh Step Prayer on the last page of journal.

Morning Review:

(Review prayers from first page).

Plan of Eating: *Today, extra food is not an option.*

Water: ☐☐☐☐☐☐☐

Breakfast:_____

_____

_____

Lunch: _____

_____

_____

Dinner: _____

_____

_____

Snack:_____

_____

_____

Gratitudes: *(A grateful heart doesn't need to eat compulsively)* *Today, I thank God for:*

_____

_____

_____

_____

_____

_____

Something I like about myself:

_____

_____

_____

_____

Something to keep in mind today:

_____

_____

_____

_____

Daily Writing: Source: _____ Pages: _____

_____

_____

_____

_____

_____

_____

_____

_____

_____

_____

_____

_____

_____

_____

Evening Review: *(or anytime the need arises)*

Today was I:

    Resentful? _____

    _____

    Selfish? _____

    _____

    Dishonest? _____

    _____

    Jealous? _____

    _____

    Fearful: (Of losing something? Of not getting what I want? Of being found out?)

    _____

    _____

    Restless, irritable or discontented? _____

    _____

Was I kind and loving towards all? _____

_____

_____

Do I owe an apology? _____

_____

_____

What did I do for others? _____

_____

_____

What could I have done better? _____

_____

_____

What did I do well? _____

_____

_____

Freedom from Bondage: Refer to the "Self Will * God's Will" chart and the "Freedom from Bondage" reading on the last pages of this journal.

God grant me freedom from _____ *and replace it with* _____

God grant me freedom from _____ *and replace it with* _____

God grant me freedom from _____ *and replace it with* _____

God grant me freedom from _____ *and replace it with* _____

God, I pray for the health, prosperity, happiness and well-being of _____

All the things I pray for myself, I pray also for _____

Review Eleventh Step Prayer on the last page of journal.

Morning Review:

(Review prayers from first page).

Plan of Eating: *Today, extra food is not an option.*

Water: ☐☐☐☐☐☐☐

Breakfast:_____

_____

_____

Lunch: _____

_____

_____

Dinner: _____

_____

_____

Snack:_____

_____

_____

Gratitudes: *(A grateful heart doesn't need to eat compulsively)*
Today, I thank God for:

_____

_____

_____

_____

_____

_____

Something I like about myself:

_____

_____

_____

_____

Something to keep in mind today:

_____

_____

_____

_____

_____

Daily Writing: Source: _____ Pages: _____

_____

_____

_____

_____

_____

_____

_____

_____

_____

_____

_____

_____

_____

_____

Su   M   Tu   W   Th   F   Sat   Date: _____ Day #:_____

Evening Review: *(or anytime the need arises)*

Today was I:

   Resentful? _____

_____

   Selfish? _____

_____

   Dishonest? _____

_____

   Jealous? _____

_____

   Fearful: (Of losing something? Of not getting what I want? Of being found out?)

_____

_____

   *Restless, irritable or discontented?*_____

_____

Was I kind and loving towards all? _____

_____

*Do I owe an apology?*_____

_____

What did I do for others? _____

_____

*What could I have done better?*_____

_____

_____

*What did I do well?*_____

_____

_____

Freedom from Bondage: Refer to the "Self Will * God's Will" chart and the "Freedom from Bondage" reading on the last pages of this journal.

God grant me freedom from _____ *and replace it with* _____
God grant me freedom from _____ *and replace it with* _____
God grant me freedom from _____ *and replace it with* _____
God grant me freedom from _____ *and replace it with* _____

*God, I pray for the health, prosperity, happiness and well-being of*_____
All the things I pray for myself, I pray also for _____

Review Eleventh Step Prayer on the last page of journal.

Morning Review:
(Review prayers from first page).

Plan of Eating: *Today, extra food is not an option.*

Water: ☐☐☐☐☐☐☐☐

Breakfast:_____
_____
_____

Lunch: _____
_____
_____

Dinner: _____
_____
_____

Snack:_____
_____
_____

Gratitudes: *(A grateful heart doesn't need to eat compulsively)* Today, I thank God for:

_____
_____
_____
_____
_____
_____

Something I like about myself:

_____
_____
_____
_____
_____

Something to keep in mind today:

_____
_____
_____
_____

Daily Writing: Source: _____ Pages: _____

_____
_____
_____
_____
_____
_____
_____
_____
_____
_____
_____
_____
_____
_____
_____

Su   M   Tu   W   Th   F   Sat   Date: _____ Day #:_____

Evening Review: *(or anytime the need arises)*

Today was I:

  Resentful? _____

    _____

  Selfish? _____

    _____

  Dishonest? _____

    _____

  Jealous? _____

    _____

  Fearful: (Of losing something? Of not getting what I want? Of being found out?)

    _____

    _____

  *Restless, irritable or discontented?*_____

    _____

Was I kind and loving towards all? _____

_____

*Do I owe an apology?*_____

_____

What did I do for others? _____

_____

*What could I have done better?*_____

_____

*What did I do well?*_____

_____

_____

Freedom from Bondage: Refer to the "Self Will * God's Will" chart and the "Freedom from Bondage" reading on the last pages of this journal.

God grant me freedom from _____ *and replace it with* _____
God grant me freedom from _____ *and replace it with* _____
God grant me freedom from _____ *and replace it with* _____
God grant me freedom from _____ *and replace it with* _____

*God, I pray for the health, prosperity, happiness and well-being of*_____
All the things I pray for myself, I pray also for _____

Review Eleventh Step Prayer on the last page of journal.

Morning Review:

(Review prayers from first page).

Plan of Eating: *Today, extra food is not an option.*

Water: ☐☐☐☐☐☐☐

Breakfast: _____
_____
_____

Lunch: _____
_____
_____

Dinner: _____
_____
_____

Snack: _____
_____
_____

Gratitudes: *(A grateful heart doesn't need to eat compulsively)*

Today, I thank God for:
_____
_____
_____
_____
_____
_____

Something I like about myself:
_____
_____
_____
_____

Something to keep in mind today:
_____
_____
_____
_____

Daily Writing: Source: _____ Pages: _____

_____
_____
_____
_____
_____
_____
_____
_____
_____
_____
_____
_____
_____
_____
_____

Su M Tu W Th F Sat   Date: _____ Day #:_____

Evening Review: *(or anytime the need arises)*

Today was I:
   Resentful?   _____

                      _____

   Selfish?   _____

                      _____

   Dishonest?   _____

                      _____

   Jealous?   _____

                      _____

   Fearful: (Of losing something? Of not getting what I want? Of being found out?)

                      _____

                      _____

   *Restless, irritable or discontented?*_____

                      _____

Was I kind and loving towards all? _____

_____

_____

Do I owe an apology? _____

_____

_____

What did I do for others? _____

_____

_____

*What could I have done better?*_____

_____

_____

*What did I do well?*_____

_____

_____

Freedom from Bondage: Refer to the "Self Will * God's Will" chart and the "Freedom from Bondage" reading on the last pages of this journal.

God grant me freedom from _____ *and replace it with* _____
God grant me freedom from _____ *and replace it with* _____
God grant me freedom from _____ *and replace it with* _____
God grant me freedom from _____ *and replace it with* _____

*God, I pray for the health, prosperity, happiness and well-being of*_____
All the things I pray for myself, I pray also for _____

Review Eleventh Step Prayer on the last page of journal.

Morning Review:

(Review prayers from first page).

Plan of Eating: *Today, extra food is not an option.*

Water: ☐☐☐☐☐☐☐

Breakfast:_____

_____

_____

Lunch: _____

_____

_____

Dinner: _____

_____

_____

Snack:_____

_____

_____

Gratitudes: *(A grateful heart doesn't need to eat compulsively)*
Today, I thank God for:

_____

_____

_____

_____

_____

_____

Something I like about myself:

_____

_____

_____

_____

Something to keep in mind today:

_____

_____

_____

_____

Daily Writing: Source: _____ Pages: _____

_____
_____
_____
_____
_____
_____
_____
_____
_____
_____
_____
_____
_____
_____

Su   M   Tu   W   Th   F   Sat   Date: _____ Day #:_____

Evening Review: *(or anytime the need arises)*

Today was I:

Resentful? _____

_____

Selfish? _____

_____

Dishonest? _____

_____

Jealous? _____

_____

Fearful: (Of losing something? Of not getting what I want? Of being found out?)

_____

_____

*Restless, irritable or discontented?*_____

_____

Was I kind and loving towards all? _____

_____

_____

*Do I owe an apology?*_____

_____

_____

What did I do for others? _____

_____

_____

*What could I have done better?*_____

_____

_____

*What did I do well?*_____

_____

_____

Freedom from Bondage: Refer to the "Self Will * God's Will" chart and the "Freedom from Bondage" reading on the last pages of this journal.

God grant me freedom from _____ *and replace it with* _____
God grant me freedom from _____ *and replace it with* _____
God grant me freedom from _____ *and replace it with* _____
God grant me freedom from _____ *and replace it with* _____

*God, I pray for the health, prosperity, happiness and well-being of*_____
All the things I pray for myself, I pray also for _____

Review Eleventh Step Prayer on the last page of journal.

Morning Review:
(Review prayers from first page).

Plan of Eating: *Today, extra food is not an option.*

Water: ☐☐☐☐☐☐☐

Breakfast:_____

_____

_____

Lunch: _____

_____

_____

Dinner: _____

_____

_____

Snack:_____

_____

_____

Gratitudes: *(A grateful heart doesn't need to eat compulsively)*
Today, I thank God for:

_____

_____

_____

_____

_____

_____

Something I like about myself:

_____

_____

_____

_____

_____

Something to keep in mind today:

_____

_____

_____

_____

_____

Daily Writing: Source: _____ Pages: _____

_____

_____

_____

_____

_____

_____

_____

_____

_____

_____

_____

_____

_____

_____

Su   M   Tu   W   Th   F   Sat   *Date:* _____ *Day #:*_____

Evening Review: *(or anytime the need arises)*

Today was I:

   Resentful? _____

_____

   Selfish? _____

_____

   Dishonest? _____

_____

   Jealous? _____

_____

   Fearful: (Of losing something? Of not getting what I want? Of being found out?)

_____

_____

   *Restless, irritable or discontented?*_____

_____

Was I kind and loving towards all? _____

_____

_____

*Do I owe an apology?*_____

_____

_____

What did I do for others? _____

_____

_____

*What could I have done better?*_____

_____

_____

*What did I do well?*_____

_____

_____

Freedom from Bondage: Refer to the "Self Will * God's Will" chart and the "Freedom from Bondage" reading on the last pages of this journal.

God grant me freedom from _____ *and replace it with* _____
God grant me freedom from _____ *and replace it with* _____
God grant me freedom from _____ *and replace it with* _____
God grant me freedom from _____ *and replace it with* _____

*God, I pray for the health, prosperity, happiness and well-being of*_____
All the things I pray for myself, I pray also for _____

Review Eleventh Step Prayer on the last page of journal.

Morning Review:

(Review prayers from first page).

Plan of Eating: *Today, extra food is not an option.*

Water: ☐☐☐☐☐☐☐☐

Breakfast:_____

_____

_____

Lunch: _____

_____

_____

Dinner: _____

_____

_____

Snack:_____

_____

_____

Gratitudes: *(A grateful heart doesn't need to eat compulsively)* *Today, I thank God for:*

_____

_____

_____

_____

_____

_____

Something I like about myself:

_____

_____

_____

_____

Something to keep in mind today:

_____

_____

_____

_____

Daily Writing: Source: _____ Pages: _____

_____

_____

_____

_____

_____

_____

_____

_____

_____

_____

_____

_____

_____

_____

Su   M   Tu   W   Th   F   Sat   Date: _____ Day #:_____

Evening Review: *(or anytime the need arises)*

Today was I:

   Resentful?   _____

                              _____

   Selfish?   _____

                              _____

   Dishonest?   _____

                              _____

   Jealous?   _____

                              _____

   Fearful: (Of losing something? Of not getting what I want? Of being found out?)

                              _____

                              _____

   Restless, irritable or discontented?_____

                              _____

Was I kind and loving towards all? _____

_____

_____

Do I owe an apology?_____

_____

_____

What did I do for others? _____

_____

_____

What could I have done better?_____

_____

_____

What did I do well?_____

_____

_____

Freedom from Bondage: Refer to the "Self Will * God's Will" chart and the "Freedom from Bondage" reading on the last pages of this journal.

God grant me freedom from _____ *and replace it with* _____

God grant me freedom from _____ *and replace it with* _____

God grant me freedom from _____ *and replace it with* _____

God grant me freedom from _____ *and replace it with* _____

*God, I pray for the health, prosperity, happiness and well-being of*_____

All the things I pray for myself, I pray also for _____

Review Eleventh Step Prayer on the last page of journal.

Morning Review:

(Review prayers from first page).

Plan of Eating: *Today, extra food is not an option.*

Water: ☐☐☐☐☐☐☐

Breakfast:_____
_____
_____

Lunch: _____
_____
_____

Dinner: _____
_____
_____

Snack:_____
_____
_____

Gratitudes: *(A grateful heart doesn't need to eat compulsively)* *Today, I thank God for:*

_____
_____
_____
_____
_____
_____

Something I like about myself:

_____
_____
_____
_____
_____

Something to keep in mind today:

_____
_____
_____
_____

Daily Writing: Source: _____ Pages: _____

_____
_____
_____
_____
_____
_____
_____
_____
_____
_____
_____
_____
_____
_____

Su   M   Tu   W   Th   F   Sat   Date: _____ Day #:_____

Evening Review: *(or anytime the need arises)*

Today was I:

Resentful?   _____

_____

Selfish?   _____

_____

Dishonest?   _____

_____

Jealous?   _____

_____

Fearful: *(Of losing something? Of not getting what I want? Of being found out?)*

_____

_____

Restless, irritable or discontented?_____

_____

Was I kind and loving towards all? _____

_____

*Do I owe an apology?*_____

_____

What did I do for others? _____

_____

*What could I have done better?*_____

_____

*What did I do well?*_____

_____

_____

Freedom from Bondage: Refer to the "Self Will * God's Will" chart and the "Freedom from Bondage" reading on the last pages of this journal.

God grant me freedom from   _____ *and replace it with* _____
God grant me freedom from   _____ *and replace it with* _____
God grant me freedom from   _____ *and replace it with* _____
God grant me freedom from   _____ *and replace it with* _____

*God, I pray for the health, prosperity, happiness and well-being of*_____
All the things I pray for myself, I pray also for _____

Review Eleventh Step Prayer on the last page of journal.

Morning Review:

(Review prayers from first page).

Plan of Eating: *Today, extra food is not an option.*

Water: ☐☐☐☐☐☐☐

Breakfast:_____
_____
_____

Lunch: _____
_____
_____

Dinner: _____
_____
_____

Snack:_____
_____
_____

Gratitudes: *(A grateful heart doesn't need to eat compulsively)* *Today, I thank God for:*

_____
_____
_____
_____
_____
_____

Something I like about myself:

_____
_____
_____
_____
_____

Something to keep in mind today:

_____
_____
_____
_____
_____

Daily Writing: Source: _____ Pages: _____

_____
_____
_____
_____
_____
_____
_____
_____
_____
_____
_____
_____
_____
_____
_____

Su   M   Tu   W   Th   F   Sat   *Date:* _____ *Day #:*_____

Evening Review: *(or anytime the need arises)*

Today was I:

   Resentful? _____

   _____

   Selfish? _____

   _____

   Dishonest? _____

   _____

   Jealous? _____

   _____

   Fearful: (Of losing something? Of not getting what I want? Of being found out?)

   _____

   _____

   Restless, irritable or discontented?_____

   _____

Was I kind and loving towards all? _____

_____

_____

*Do I owe an apology?*_____

_____

_____

What did I do for others? _____

_____

_____

*What could I have done better?*_____

_____

_____

*What did I do well?*_____

_____

_____

Freedom from Bondage: Refer to the "Self Will * God's Will" chart and the "Freedom from Bondage" reading on the last pages of this journal.

God grant me freedom from _____ *and replace it with* _____
God grant me freedom from _____ *and replace it with* _____
God grant me freedom from _____ *and replace it with* _____
God grant me freedom from _____ *and replace it with* _____

*God, I pray for the health, prosperity, happiness and well-being of*_____
All the things I pray for myself, I pray also for _____

Review Eleventh Step Prayer on the last page of journal.

Morning Review:
(*Review prayers from first page*).

Plan of Eating: *Today, extra food is not an option.*

Water: ☐☐☐☐☐☐☐

Breakfast:_____
_____
_____

Lunch: _____
_____
_____

Dinner: _____
_____
_____

Snack:_____
_____
_____

Gratitudes: (*A grateful heart doesn't need to eat compulsively*) *Today, I thank God for*:

_____
_____
_____
_____
_____
_____

Something I like about myself:

_____
_____
_____
_____

Something to keep in mind today:

_____
_____
_____
_____
_____

Daily Writing: Source: _____ Pages: _____

_____
_____
_____
_____
_____
_____
_____
_____
_____
_____
_____
_____
_____
_____
_____

Su   M   Tu   W   Th   F   Sat   Date: _____ Day #:_____

Evening Review: *(or anytime the need arises)*

Today was I:

   Resentful? _____

   _____

   Selfish? _____

   _____

   Dishonest? _____

   _____

   Jealous? _____

   _____

   Fearful: (Of losing something? Of not getting what I want? Of being found out?)

   _____

   _____

   *Restless, irritable or discontented?*_____

   _____

Was I kind and loving towards all? _____

_____

_____

*Do I owe an apology?*_____

_____

_____

What did I do for others? _____

_____

_____

*What could I have done better?*_____

_____

_____

*What did I do well?*_____

_____

_____

Freedom from Bondage: Refer to the "Self Will * God's Will" chart and the "Freedom from Bondage" reading on the last pages of this journal.

God grant me freedom from _____ *and replace it with* _____
God grant me freedom from _____ *and replace it with* _____
God grant me freedom from _____ *and replace it with* _____
God grant me freedom from _____ *and replace it with* _____

*God, I pray for the health, prosperity, happiness and well-being of*_____
All the things I pray for myself, I pray also for _____

Review Eleventh Step Prayer on the last page of journal.

Morning Review:

(*Review prayers from first page*).

Plan of Eating: *Today, extra food is not an option.*

Water: ☐☐☐☐☐☐☐☐

Breakfast:_____

_____

_____

Lunch: _____

_____

_____

Dinner: _____

_____

_____

Snack:_____

_____

_____

Gratitudes: (*A grateful heart doesn't need to eat compulsively*) *Today, I thank God for*:

_____

_____

_____

_____

_____

_____

Something I like about myself:

_____

_____

_____

_____

Something to keep in mind today:

_____

_____

_____

_____

_____

Daily Writing: Source: _____ Pages: _____

_____

_____

_____

_____

_____

_____

_____

_____

_____

_____

_____

_____

_____

_____

Su   M   Tu   W   Th   F   Sat   Date: _____ Day #:_____

Evening Review: *(or anytime the need arises)*

Today was I:

   Resentful? _____

_____

   Selfish? _____

_____

   Dishonest? _____

_____

   Jealous? _____

_____

   Fearful: (Of losing something? Of not getting what I want? Of being found out?)

_____

_____

   *Restless, irritable or discontented?*_____

_____

Was I kind and loving towards all? _____

_____

_____

*Do I owe an apology?*_____

_____

_____

What did I do for others? _____

_____

_____

*What could I have done better?*_____

_____

_____

*What did I do well?*_____

_____

_____

Freedom from Bondage: Refer to the "Self Will * God's Will" chart and the "Freedom from Bondage" reading on the last pages of this journal.

God grant me freedom from _____ *and replace it with* _____
God grant me freedom from _____ *and replace it with* _____
God grant me freedom from _____ *and replace it with* _____
God grant me freedom from _____ *and replace it with* _____

*God, I pray for the health, prosperity, happiness and well-being of*_____
All the things I pray for myself, I pray also for _____

Review Eleventh Step Prayer on the last page of journal.

Morning Review:
(Review prayers from first page).

Plan of Eating: *Today, extra food is not an option.*

Water: □□□□□□□

Breakfast:_____
_____
_____

Lunch: _____
_____
_____

Dinner: _____
_____
_____

Snack:_____
_____
_____

Gratitudes: *(A grateful heart doesn't need to eat compulsively)*
Today, I thank God for:

_____
_____
_____
_____
_____
_____

Something I like about myself:

_____
_____
_____
_____
_____

Something to keep in mind today:

_____
_____
_____
_____
_____

Daily Writing: Source: _____ Pages: _____

_____
_____
_____
_____
_____
_____
_____
_____
_____
_____
_____
_____
_____

Su M Tu W Th F Sat   Date: _____ Day #:_____

Evening Review: *(or anytime the need arises)*

Today was I:

   Resentful?   _____

   _____

   Selfish?   _____

   _____

   Dishonest?   _____

   _____

   Jealous?   _____

   _____

   Fearful: (Of losing something? Of not getting what I want? Of being found out?)

   _____

   _____

   Restless, irritable or discontented?_____

   _____

Was I kind and loving towards all? _____

_____

_____

*Do I owe an apology?*_____

_____

_____

What did I do for others? _____

_____

_____

*What could I have done better?*_____

_____

_____

*What did I do well?*_____

_____

_____

Freedom from Bondage: Refer to the "Self Will * God's Will" chart and the "Freedom from Bondage" reading on the last pages of this journal.

God grant me freedom from _____ *and replace it with* _____
God grant me freedom from _____ *and replace it with* _____
God grant me freedom from _____ *and replace it with* _____
God grant me freedom from _____ *and replace it with* _____

*God, I pray for the health, prosperity, happiness and well-being of*_____
All the things I pray for myself, I pray also for _____

Review Eleventh Step Prayer on the last page of journal.

Morning Review:
(*Review prayers from first page*).

Plan of Eating: *Today, extra food is not an option.*

Water: ☐☐☐☐☐☐☐

Breakfast:_____
_____
_____

Lunch: _____
_____
_____

Dinner: _____
_____
_____

Snack:_____
_____
_____

Gratitudes: (*A grateful heart doesn't need to eat compulsively*) *Today, I thank God for*:

_____
_____
_____
_____
_____
_____

Something I like about myself:

_____
_____
_____
_____

Something to keep in mind today:

_____
_____
_____
_____

Daily Writing: Source: _____ Pages: _____

_____
_____
_____
_____
_____
_____
_____
_____
_____
_____
_____
_____
_____
_____

Su   M   Tu   W   Th   F   Sat   Date: _____ Day #:_____

Evening Review: *(or anytime the need arises)*

Today was I:

   Resentful? _____

_____

   Selfish? _____

_____

   Dishonest? _____

_____

   Jealous? _____

_____

   Fearful: (Of losing something? Of not getting what I want? Of being found out?)

_____

_____

   *Restless, irritable or discontented?*_____

_____

Was I kind and loving towards all? _____

_____

_____

*Do I owe an apology?*_____

_____

_____

What did I do for others? _____

_____

_____

*What could I have done better?*_____

_____

_____

*What did I do well?*_____

_____

_____

Freedom from Bondage: Refer to the "Self Will * God's Will" chart and the "Freedom from Bondage" reading on the last pages of this journal.

God grant me freedom from _____ *and replace it with* _____
God grant me freedom from _____ *and replace it with* _____
God grant me freedom from _____ *and replace it with* _____
God grant me freedom from _____ *and replace it with* _____

*God, I pray for the health, prosperity, happiness and well-being of*_____
All the things I pray for myself, I pray also for _____

Review Eleventh Step Prayer on the last page of journal.

Morning Review:
(Review prayers from first page).

Plan of Eating: *Today, extra food is not an option.*

Water: ☐☐☐☐☐☐☐☐

Breakfast:_____
_____
_____

Lunch: _____
_____
_____

Dinner: _____
_____
_____

Snack:_____
_____
_____

Gratitudes: *(A grateful heart doesn't need to eat compulsively)* Today, I thank God for:
_____
_____
_____
_____
_____
_____

Something I like about myself:
_____
_____
_____
_____

Something to keep in mind today:
_____
_____
_____
_____

Daily Writing: Source: _____ Pages: _____
_____
_____
_____
_____
_____
_____
_____
_____
_____
_____
_____
_____
_____
_____

Su   M   Tu   W   Th   F   Sat   Date: _____ Day #:_____

Evening Review: *(or anytime the need arises)*

Today was I:

   Resentful? _____

   _____

   Selfish? _____

   _____

   Dishonest? _____

   _____

   Jealous? _____

   Fearful: (Of losing something? Of not getting what I want? Of being found out?)

   _____

   _____

   *Restless, irritable or discontented?*_____

   _____

Was I kind and loving towards all? _____

_____

_____

*Do I owe an apology?*_____

_____

_____

What did I do for others? _____

_____

_____

*What could I have done better?*_____

_____

_____

*What did I do well?*_____

_____

_____

Freedom from Bondage: Refer to the "Self Will * God's Will" chart and the "Freedom from Bondage" reading on the last pages of this journal.

God grant me freedom from _____ *and replace it with* _____
God grant me freedom from _____ *and replace it with* _____
God grant me freedom from _____ *and replace it with* _____
God grant me freedom from _____ *and replace it with* _____

*God, I pray for the health, prosperity, happiness and well-being of*_____
All the things I pray for myself, I pray also for _____

Review Eleventh Step Prayer on the last page of journal.

Morning Review:
(Review prayers from first page).

Plan of Eating: *Today, extra food is not an option.*

Water: ⬜⬜⬜⬜⬜⬜⬜

Breakfast:_____

_____

_____

Lunch: _____

_____

_____

Dinner: _____

_____

_____

Snack:_____

_____

_____

Gratitudes: *(A grateful heart doesn't need to eat compulsively)*
Today, I thank God for:

_____

_____

_____

_____

_____

_____

Something I like about myself:

_____

_____

_____

_____

_____

Something to keep in mind today:

_____

_____

_____

_____

Daily Writing: Source: _____ Pages: _____

_____

_____

_____

_____

_____

_____

_____

_____

_____

_____

_____

_____

_____

_____

Evening Review: *(or anytime the need arises)*

Today was I:

  Resentful? _____

  _____

  Selfish? _____

  _____

  Dishonest? _____

  _____

  Jealous? _____

  _____

  Fearful: (Of losing something? Of not getting what I want? Of being found out?)

  _____

  _____

  *Restless, irritable or discontented?*_____

  _____

Was I kind and loving towards all? _____

_____

_____

*Do I owe an apology?*_____

_____

_____

*What did I do for others?*_____

_____

_____

*What could I have done better?*_____

_____

_____

*What did I do well?*_____

_____

_____

Freedom from Bondage: Refer to the "Self Will * God's Will" chart and the "Freedom from Bondage" reading on the last pages of this journal.

God grant me freedom from   _____   *and replace it with* _____
God grant me freedom from   _____   *and replace it with* _____
God grant me freedom from   _____   *and replace it with* _____
God grant me freedom from   _____   *and replace it with* _____

*God, I pray for the health, prosperity, happiness and well-being of*_____
All the things I pray for myself, I pray also for _____

Review Eleventh Step Prayer on the last page of journal.

Morning Review:

(Review prayers from first page).

Plan of Eating: *Today, extra food is not an option.*

Water: ☐☐☐☐☐☐☐

Breakfast:_____
_____
_____

Lunch: _____
_____
_____

Dinner: _____
_____
_____

Snack:_____
_____
_____

Gratitudes: *(A grateful heart doesn't need to eat compulsively)* *Today, I thank God for:*

_____
_____
_____
_____
_____
_____

Something I like about myself:

_____
_____
_____
_____
_____

Something to keep in mind today:

_____
_____
_____
_____
_____

Daily Writing: Source: _____ Pages: _____

_____
_____
_____
_____
_____
_____
_____
_____
_____
_____
_____
_____
_____
_____
_____

Su   M   Tu   W   Th   F   Sat   Date: _____   Day #:_____

Evening Review: *(or anytime the need arises)*

Today was I:

   Resentful? _____

   _____

   Selfish? _____

   _____

   Dishonest? _____

   _____

   Jealous? _____

   _____

   Fearful: (Of losing something? Of not getting what I want? Of being found out?)

   _____

   _____

   Restless, irritable or discontented? _____

   _____

Was I kind and loving towards all? _____

_____

_____

Do I owe an apology? _____

_____

_____

What did I do for others? _____

_____

_____

What could I have done better? _____

_____

_____

What did I do well? _____

_____

_____

Freedom from Bondage: Refer to the "Self Will * God's Will" chart and the "Freedom from Bondage" reading on the last pages of this journal.

God grant me freedom from _____ *and replace it with* _____
God grant me freedom from _____ *and replace it with* _____
God grant me freedom from _____ *and replace it with* _____
God grant me freedom from _____ *and replace it with* _____

God, I pray for the health, prosperity, happiness and well-being of _____
All the things I pray for myself, I pray also for _____

Review Eleventh Step Prayer on the last page of journal.

Morning Review:

(Review prayers from first page).

Plan of Eating: *Today, extra food is not an option.*

Water: ☐☐☐☐☐☐☐

Breakfast:_____

_____

_____

Lunch: _____

_____

_____

Dinner: _____

_____

_____

Snack:_____

_____

_____

Gratitudes: *(A grateful heart doesn't need to eat compulsively)*
Today, I thank God for:

_____

_____

_____

_____

_____

_____

Something I like about myself:

_____

_____

_____

_____

_____

Something to keep in mind today:

_____

_____

_____

_____

_____

Daily Writing: Source: _____ Pages: _____

_____

_____

_____

_____

_____

_____

_____

_____

_____

_____

_____

_____

_____

_____

_____

Su   M   Tu   W   Th   F   Sat   Date: _____ Day #:_____

Evening Review: *(or anytime the need arises)*

Today was I:

   Resentful?   _____

   _____

   Selfish?   _____

   _____

   Dishonest?   _____

   _____

   Jealous?   _____

   _____

   Fearful: (Of losing something? Of not getting what I want? Of being found out?)

   _____

   _____

   Restless, irritable or discontented?_____

   _____

Was I kind and loving towards all? _____

_____

_____

Do I owe an apology?_____

_____

_____

What did I do for others? _____

_____

_____

What could I have done better?_____

_____

_____

What did I do well?_____

_____

_____

Freedom from Bondage: Refer to the "Self Will * God's Will" chart and the "Freedom from Bondage" reading on the last pages of this journal.

God grant me freedom from _____ *and replace it with* _____
God grant me freedom from _____ *and replace it with* _____
God grant me freedom from _____ *and replace it with* _____
God grant me freedom from _____ *and replace it with* _____

God, I pray for the health, prosperity, happiness and well-being of_____
All the things I pray for myself, I pray also for _____

Review Eleventh Step Prayer on the last page of journal.

Morning Review:
(*Review prayers from first page*).

Plan of Eating: *Today, extra food is not an option.*

Water: ☐☐☐☐☐☐☐

Breakfast:_____
_____
_____

Lunch: _____
_____
_____

Dinner: _____
_____
_____

Snack:_____
_____
_____

Gratitudes: (*A grateful heart doesn't need to eat compulsively*)
Today, I thank God for:

_____
_____
_____
_____
_____
_____

Something I like about myself:

_____
_____
_____
_____
_____

Something to keep in mind today:

_____
_____
_____
_____
_____

Daily Writing: Source: _____ Pages: _____

_____
_____
_____
_____
_____
_____
_____
_____
_____
_____
_____
_____
_____
_____
_____

Su M Tu W Th F Sat   Date: _____ Day #:_____

Evening Review: *(or anytime the need arises)*

Today was I:

   Resentful?   _____

                       _____

   Selfish?   _____

                       _____

   Dishonest?   _____

                       _____

   Jealous?   _____

                       _____

   Fearful: (Of losing something? Of not getting what I want? Of being found out?)

                       _____

                       _____

   Restless, irritable or discontented?_____

                       _____

Was I kind and loving towards all? _____

_____

_____

Do I owe an apology?_____

_____

_____

What did I do for others? _____

_____

_____

What could I have done better?_____

_____

_____

What did I do well?_____

_____

_____

Freedom from Bondage: Refer to the "Self Will * God's Will" chart and the "Freedom from Bondage" reading on the last pages of this journal.

God grant me freedom from _____ *and replace it with* _____
God grant me freedom from _____ *and replace it with* _____
God grant me freedom from _____ *and replace it with* _____
God grant me freedom from _____ *and replace it with* _____

God, I pray for the health, prosperity, happiness and well-being of_____
All the things I pray for myself, I pray also for _____

Review Eleventh Step Prayer on the last page of journal.

Morning Review:
(*Review prayers from first page*).

Plan of Eating: *Today, extra food is not an option.*

Water: ☐☐☐☐☐☐☐

Breakfast:_____
_____
_____

Lunch: _____
_____
_____

Dinner: _____
_____
_____

Snack:_____
_____
_____

Gratitudes: (*A grateful heart doesn't need to eat compulsively*) Today, I thank God for:

_____
_____
_____
_____
_____
_____

Something I like about myself:

_____
_____
_____
_____
_____

Something to keep in mind today:

_____
_____
_____
_____

Daily Writing: Source: _____ Pages: _____

_____
_____
_____
_____
_____
_____
_____
_____
_____
_____
_____
_____
_____
_____
_____

Su M Tu W Th F Sat   Date: _____ Day #:_____

Evening Review: *(or anytime the need arises)*

Today was I:

Resentful? _____

_____

Selfish? _____

_____

Dishonest? _____

_____

Jealous? _____

_____

Fearful: (Of losing something? Of not getting what I want? Of being found out?)

_____

_____

*Restless, irritable or discontented?*_____

_____

Was I kind and loving towards all? _____

_____

*Do I owe an apology?*_____

_____

What did I do for others? _____

_____

*What could I have done better?*_____

_____

_____

*What did I do well?*_____

_____

_____

Freedom from Bondage: Refer to the "Self Will * God's Will" chart and the
"Freedom from Bondage" reading on the last pages of this journal.

God grant me freedom from _____ *and replace it with* _____
God grant me freedom from _____ *and replace it with* _____
God grant me freedom from _____ *and replace it with* _____
God grant me freedom from _____ *and replace it with* _____

*God, I pray for the health, prosperity, happiness and well-being of*_____
All the things I pray for myself, I pray also for _____

Review Eleventh Step Prayer on the last page of journal.

Morning Review:

(Review prayers from first page).

Plan of Eating: *Today, extra food is not an option.*

Water: ☐☐☐☐☐☐☐

Breakfast:_____

_____

_____

Lunch: _____

_____

_____

Dinner: _____

_____

_____

Snack:_____

_____

_____

Gratitudes: *(A grateful heart doesn't need to eat compulsively) Today, I thank God for:*

_____

_____

_____

_____

_____

_____

Something I like about myself:

_____

_____

_____

_____

_____

Something to keep in mind today:

_____

_____

_____

_____

_____

Daily Writing: Source: _____ Pages: _____

_____

_____

_____

_____

_____

_____

_____

_____

_____

_____

_____

_____

_____

_____

_____

Su   M   Tu   W   Th   F   Sat   Date: _____   Day #:_____

Evening Review: *(or anytime the need arises)*

Today was I:

   Resentful?   _____

                     _____

   Selfish?   _____

                     _____

   Dishonest?   _____

                     _____

   Jealous?   _____

                     _____

   Fearful: (Of losing something? Of not getting what I want? Of being found out?)

                     _____

                     _____

   Restless, irritable or discontented?_____

                     _____

Was I kind and loving towards all? _____

_____

_____

*Do I owe an apology?*_____

_____

_____

What did I do for others? _____

_____

_____

*What could I have done better?*_____

_____

_____

*What did I do well?*_____

_____

_____

Freedom from Bondage: Refer to the "Self Will * God's Will" chart and the "Freedom from Bondage" reading on the last pages of this journal.

God grant me freedom from _____ *and replace it with* _____

God grant me freedom from _____ *and replace it with* _____

God grant me freedom from _____ *and replace it with* _____

God grant me freedom from _____ *and replace it with* _____

*God, I pray for the health, prosperity, happiness and well-being of*_____

All the things I pray for myself, I pray also for _____

Review Eleventh Step Prayer on the last page of journal.

Morning Review:
(Review prayers from first page).

Plan of Eating: *Today, extra food is not an option.*

Water: ☐☐☐☐☐☐☐

Breakfast:_____
_____
_____

Lunch: _____
_____
_____

Dinner: _____
_____
_____

Snack:_____
_____
_____

Gratitudes: (*A grateful heart doesn't need to eat compulsively*)
Today, I thank God for:

_____
_____
_____
_____
_____
_____

Something I like about myself:

_____
_____
_____
_____
_____

Something to keep in mind today:

_____
_____
_____
_____

Daily Writing: Source: _____ Pages: _____

_____
_____
_____
_____
_____
_____
_____
_____
_____
_____
_____
_____
_____
_____

Evening Review: *(or anytime the need arises)*

Today was I:

Resentful?   _____

_____

Selfish?   _____

_____

Dishonest?   _____

_____

Jealous?   _____

_____

Fearful: (Of losing something? Of not getting what I want? Of being found out?)

_____

_____

*Restless, irritable or discontented?*_____

_____

Was I kind and loving towards all? _____

_____

*Do I owe an apology?*_____

_____

What did I do for others? _____

_____

*What could I have done better?*_____

_____

*What did I do well?*_____

_____

_____

Freedom from Bondage: Refer to the "Self Will * God's Will" chart and the "Freedom from Bondage" reading on the last pages of this journal.

God grant me freedom from _____ *and replace it with* _____
God grant me freedom from _____ *and replace it with* _____
God grant me freedom from _____ *and replace it with* _____
God grant me freedom from _____ *and replace it with* _____

*God, I pray for the health, prosperity, happiness and well-being of*_____
All the things I pray for myself, I pray also for _____

Review Eleventh Step Prayer on the last page of journal.

Morning Review:

(Review prayers from first page).

Plan of Eating: *Today, extra food is not an option.*

Water: ☐☐☐☐☐☐☐

Breakfast:_____
_____
_____

Lunch: _____
_____
_____

Dinner: _____
_____
_____

Snack:_____
_____
_____

Gratitudes: *(A grateful heart doesn't need to eat compulsively)* Today, I thank God for:

_____
_____
_____
_____
_____
_____

Something I like about myself:

_____
_____
_____
_____
_____

Something to keep in mind today:

_____
_____
_____
_____

Daily Writing: Source: _____ Pages: _____

_____
_____
_____
_____
_____
_____
_____
_____
_____
_____
_____
_____
_____
_____
_____
_____

Evening Review: *(or anytime the need arises)*

Today was I:

Resentful?   _____

_____

Selfish?   _____

_____

Dishonest?   _____

_____

Jealous?   _____

_____

Fearful: (Of losing something? Of not getting what I want? Of being found out?)

_____

_____

Restless, irritable or discontented?_____

_____

Was I kind and loving towards all? _____

_____

_____

Do I owe an apology?_____

_____

_____

What did I do for others? _____

_____

_____

What could I have done better?_____

_____

_____

What did I do well?_____

_____

_____

Freedom from Bondage: Refer to the "Self Will * God's Will" chart and the "Freedom from Bondage" reading on the last pages of this journal.

God grant me freedom from _____ *and replace it with* _____
God grant me freedom from _____ *and replace it with* _____
God grant me freedom from _____ *and replace it with* _____
God grant me freedom from _____ *and replace it with* _____

God, I pray for the health, prosperity, happiness and well-being of_____
All the things I pray for myself, I pray also for _____

Review Eleventh Step Prayer on the last page of journal.

Morning Review:

(Review prayers from first page).

Plan of Eating: *Today, extra food is not an option.*

Water: ☐☐☐☐☐☐☐

Breakfast:_____
_____
_____

Lunch: _____
_____
_____

Dinner: _____
_____
_____

Snack:_____
_____
_____

Gratitudes: *(A grateful heart doesn't need to eat compulsively)* *Today, I thank God for:*

_____
_____
_____
_____
_____
_____

Something I like about myself:

_____
_____
_____
_____

Something to keep in mind today:

_____
_____
_____
_____

Daily Writing: Source: _____ Pages: _____

_____
_____
_____
_____
_____
_____
_____
_____
_____
_____
_____
_____
_____
_____
_____

Su   M   Tu   W   Th   F   Sat   Date: _____   Day #:_____

Evening Review: *(or anytime the need arises)*

Today was I:

   Resentful?   _____

                        _____

   Selfish?   _____

                        _____

   Dishonest?   _____

                        _____

   Jealous?   _____

                        _____

   Fearful: (Of losing something? Of not getting what I want? Of being found out?)

                        _____

                        _____

   Restless, irritable or discontented?_____

                        _____

Was I kind and loving towards all? _____

_____

_____

*Do I owe an apology?*_____

_____

_____

What did I do for others? _____

_____

_____

*What could I have done better?*_____

_____

_____

*What did I do well?*_____

_____

_____

Freedom from Bondage: Refer to the "Self Will * God's Will" chart and the "Freedom from Bondage" reading on the last pages of this journal.

God grant me freedom from _____ *and replace it with* _____

God grant me freedom from _____ *and replace it with* _____

God grant me freedom from _____ *and replace it with* _____

God grant me freedom from _____ *and replace it with* _____

*God, I pray for the health, prosperity, happiness and well-being of*_____

All the things I pray for myself, I pray also for _____

Review Eleventh Step Prayer on the last page of journal.

Morning Review:
(Review prayers from first page).

Plan of Eating: *Today, extra food is not an option.*

Water: ☐☐☐☐☐☐☐

Breakfast:_____
_____
_____

Lunch: _____
_____
_____

Dinner: _____
_____
_____

Snack:_____
_____
_____

Gratitudes: *(A grateful heart doesn't need to eat compulsively)*
Today, I thank God for:

_____
_____
_____
_____
_____
_____

Something I like about myself:

_____
_____
_____
_____
_____

Something to keep in mind today:

_____
_____
_____
_____
_____

Daily Writing: Source: _____ Pages: _____

_____
_____
_____
_____
_____
_____
_____
_____
_____
_____
_____
_____
_____
_____

Su   M   Tu   W   Th   F   Sat   Date: _____ Day #:_____

Evening Review: *(or anytime the need arises)*

Today was I:

    Resentful? _____

    _____

    Selfish? _____

    _____

    Dishonest? _____

    _____

    Jealous? _____

    _____

    Fearful: (Of losing something? Of not getting what I want? Of being found out?)

    _____

    _____

    *Restless, irritable or discontented?*_____

    _____

Was I kind and loving towards all? _____

_____

_____

*Do I owe an apology?*_____

_____

_____

What did I do for others? _____

_____

_____

*What could I have done better?*_____

_____

_____

*What did I do well?*_____

_____

_____

Freedom from Bondage: Refer to the "Self Will * God's Will" chart and the "Freedom from Bondage" reading on the last pages of this journal.

God grant me freedom from _____ *and replace it with* _____
God grant me freedom from _____ *and replace it with* _____
God grant me freedom from _____ *and replace it with* _____
God grant me freedom from _____ *and replace it with* _____

*God, I pray for the health, prosperity, happiness and well-being of*_____
All the things I pray for myself, I pray also for _____

Review Eleventh Step Prayer on the last page of journal.

Morning Review:
(*Review prayers from first page*).

Plan of Eating: *Today, extra food is not an option.*

Water: ⬜⬜⬜⬜⬜⬜⬜

Breakfast:_____
_____
_____

Lunch: _____
_____
_____

Dinner: _____
_____
_____

Snack:_____
_____
_____

Gratitudes: (*A grateful heart doesn't need to eat compulsively*) *Today, I thank God for:*

_____
_____
_____
_____
_____
_____

Something I like about myself:

_____
_____
_____
_____

Something to keep in mind today:

_____
_____
_____
_____

Daily Writing: Source: _____ Pages: _____

_____
_____
_____
_____
_____
_____
_____
_____
_____
_____
_____
_____
_____
_____

Evening Review: *(or anytime the need arises)*

Today was I:

Resentful?   _____

_____

Selfish?   _____

_____

Dishonest?   _____

_____

Jealous?   _____

_____

Fearful: (Of losing something? Of not getting what I want? Of being found out?)

_____

_____

Restless, irritable or discontented?_____

_____

Was I kind and loving towards all? _____

_____

_____

Do I owe an apology?_____

_____

_____

What did I do for others? _____

_____

_____

What could I have done better?_____

_____

_____

What did I do well?_____

_____

_____

Freedom from Bondage: Refer to the "Self Will * God's Will" chart and the "Freedom from Bondage" reading on the last pages of this journal.

God grant me freedom from _____ *and replace it with* _____

God grant me freedom from _____ *and replace it with* _____

God grant me freedom from _____ *and replace it with* _____

God grant me freedom from _____ *and replace it with* _____

*God, I pray for the health, prosperity, happiness and well-being of*_____

All the things I pray for myself, I pray also for _____

Review Eleventh Step Prayer on the last page of journal.

Morning Review:

(Review prayers from first page).

Plan of Eating: *Today, extra food is not an option.*

Water: ☐☐☐☐☐☐☐

Breakfast:_____

_____

_____

Lunch: _____

_____

_____

Dinner: _____

_____

_____

Snack:_____

_____

_____

Gratitudes: *(A grateful heart doesn't need to eat compulsively)*
Today, I thank God for:

_____

_____

_____

_____

_____

_____

Something I like about myself:

_____

_____

_____

_____

_____

Something to keep in mind today:

_____

_____

_____

_____

_____

Daily Writing: Source: _____ Pages: _____

_____

_____

_____

_____

_____

_____

_____

_____

_____

_____

_____

_____

_____

_____

_____

_____

Su M Tu W Th F Sat   Date: _____ Day #:_____

Evening Review: *(or anytime the need arises)*

Today was I:

   Resentful? _____

   _____

   Selfish? _____

   _____

   Dishonest? _____

   _____

   Jealous? _____

   _____

   Fearful: (Of losing something? Of not getting what I want? Of being found out?)

   _____

   _____

   *Restless, irritable or discontented?*_____

   _____

Was I kind and loving towards all? _____

_____

_____

*Do I owe an apology?*_____

_____

_____

What did I do for others? _____

_____

_____

*What could I have done better?*_____

_____

_____

*What did I do well?*_____

_____

_____

Freedom from Bondage: Refer to the "Self Will * God's Will" chart and the "Freedom from Bondage" reading on the last pages of this journal.

God grant me freedom from _____ *and replace it with* _____
God grant me freedom from _____ *and replace it with* _____
God grant me freedom from _____ *and replace it with* _____
God grant me freedom from _____ *and replace it with* _____

*God, I pray for the health, prosperity, happiness and well-being of*_____
All the things I pray for myself, I pray also for _____

Review Eleventh Step Prayer on the last page of journal.

Morning Review:
(*Review prayers from first page*).

Plan of Eating: *Today, extra food is not an option.*

Water: ☐☐☐☐☐☐☐

Breakfast:_____
_____
_____

Lunch: _____
_____
_____

Dinner: _____
_____
_____

Snack:_____
_____
_____

Gratitudes: (*A grateful heart doesn't need to eat compulsively*)
Today, I thank God for:
_____
_____
_____
_____
_____
_____

Something I like about myself:
_____
_____
_____
_____
_____

Something to keep in mind today:
_____
_____
_____
_____
_____

Daily Writing: Source: _____ Pages: _____
_____
_____
_____
_____
_____
_____
_____
_____
_____
_____
_____
_____
_____
_____
_____

Su   M   Tu   W   Th   F   Sat   Date: _____ Day #:_____

Evening Review: *(or anytime the need arises)*

Today was I:

   Resentful?   _____

                        _____

   Selfish?   _____

                        _____

   Dishonest?   _____

                        _____

   Jealous?   _____

                        _____

   Fearful: (Of losing something? Of not getting what I want? Of being found out?)

                        _____

                        _____

   *Restless, irritable or discontented?*_____

                        _____

Was I kind and loving towards all? _____

_____

_____

*Do I owe an apology?*_____

_____

_____

What did I do for others? _____

_____

_____

*What could I have done better?*_____

_____

_____

*What did I do well?*_____

_____

_____

Freedom from Bondage: Refer to the "Self Will * God's Will" chart and the "Freedom from Bondage" reading on the last pages of this journal.

God grant me freedom from _____ *and replace it with* _____
God grant me freedom from _____ *and replace it with* _____
God grant me freedom from _____ *and replace it with* _____
God grant me freedom from _____ *and replace it with* _____

*God, I pray for the health, prosperity, happiness and well-being of*_____
All the things I pray for myself, I pray also for _____

Review Eleventh Step Prayer on the last page of journal.

Morning Review:

(Review prayers from first page).

Plan of Eating: *Today, extra food is not an option.*

Water: ⬜⬜⬜⬜⬜⬜⬜

Breakfast:_____

_____

_____

Lunch: _____

_____

_____

Dinner: _____

_____

_____

Snack:_____

_____

_____

Gratitudes: *(A grateful heart doesn't need to eat compulsively)* Today, I thank God for:

_____

_____

_____

_____

_____

_____

Something I like about myself:

_____

_____

_____

_____

_____

Something to keep in mind today:

_____

_____

_____

_____

Daily Writing: Source: _____ Pages: _____

_____

_____

_____

_____

_____

_____

_____

_____

_____

_____

_____

_____

_____

_____

Su   M   Tu   W   Th   F   Sat   Date: _____ Day #:_____

Evening Review: *(or anytime the need arises)*

Today was I:

    Resentful? _____

_____

    Selfish? _____

_____

    Dishonest? _____

_____

    Jealous? _____

_____

    Fearful: (Of losing something? Of not getting what I want? Of being found out?)

_____

_____

    Restless, irritable or discontented? _____

_____

Was I kind and loving towards all? _____

_____

_____

Do I owe an apology? _____

_____

_____

What did I do for others? _____

_____

_____

What could I have done better? _____

_____

_____

What did I do well? _____

_____

_____

Freedom from Bondage: Refer to the "Self Will * God's Will" chart and the "Freedom from Bondage" reading on the last pages of this journal.

God grant me freedom from _____ *and replace it with* _____
God grant me freedom from _____ *and replace it with* _____
God grant me freedom from _____ *and replace it with* _____
God grant me freedom from _____ *and replace it with* _____

God, I pray for the health, prosperity, happiness and well-being of _____
All the things I pray for myself, I pray also for _____

Review Eleventh Step Prayer on the last page of journal.

Morning Review:

(*Review prayers from first page*).

Plan of Eating: *Today, extra food is not an option.*

Water: ☐☐☐☐☐☐☐☐

Breakfast:_____

_____

_____

Lunch: _____

_____

_____

Dinner: _____

_____

_____

Snack:_____

_____

_____

Gratitudes: (*A grateful heart doesn't need to eat compulsively*) *Today, I thank God for*:

_____

_____

_____

_____

_____

_____

Something I like about myself:

_____

_____

_____

_____

Something to keep in mind today:

_____

_____

_____

_____

Daily Writing: Source: _____ Pages: _____

_____

_____

_____

_____

_____

_____

_____

_____

_____

_____

_____

_____

_____

Su   M   Tu   W   Th   F   Sat   Date: _____ Day #:_____

Evening Review: *(or anytime the need arises)*

Today was I:

Resentful?   _____

_____

Selfish?   _____

_____

Dishonest?   _____

_____

Jealous?   _____

_____

Fearful: (Of losing something? Of not getting what I want? Of being found out?)

_____

_____

*Restless, irritable or discontented?*_____

_____

Was I kind and loving towards all? _____

_____

_____

*Do I owe an apology?*_____

_____

_____

What did I do for others? _____

_____

_____

*What could I have done better?*_____

_____

_____

*What did I do well?*_____

_____

_____

Freedom from Bondage: Refer to the "Self Will * God's Will" chart and the "Freedom from Bondage" reading on the last pages of this journal.

God grant me freedom from _____ *and replace it with* _____
God grant me freedom from _____ *and replace it with* _____
God grant me freedom from _____ *and replace it with* _____
God grant me freedom from _____ *and replace it with* _____

*God, I pray for the health, prosperity, happiness and well-being of*_____
All the things I pray for myself, I pray also for _____

Review Eleventh Step Prayer on the last page of journal.

Morning Review:

(Review prayers from first page).

Plan of Eating: *Today, extra food is not an option.*

Water: ☐☐☐☐☐☐☐

Breakfast:_____

_____

_____

Lunch: _____

_____

_____

Dinner: _____

_____

_____

Snack:_____

_____

_____

Gratitudes: *(A grateful heart doesn't need to eat compulsively)* Today, I thank God for:

_____

_____

_____

_____

_____

_____

Something I like about myself:

_____

_____

_____

_____

_____

Something to keep in mind today:

_____

_____

_____

_____

_____

Daily Writing: Source: _____ Pages: _____

_____

_____

_____

_____

_____

_____

_____

_____

_____

_____

_____

_____

_____

_____

Su   M   Tu   W   Th   F   Sat   *Date:* _____ *Day #:*_____

Evening Review: *(or anytime the need arises)*

Today was I:

   Resentful? _____

_____

   Selfish? _____

_____

   Dishonest? _____

_____

   Jealous? _____

_____

   Fearful: (Of losing something? Of not getting what I want? Of being found out?)

_____

_____

   *Restless, irritable or discontented?*_____

_____

Was I kind and loving towards all? _____

_____

_____

*Do I owe an apology?*_____

_____

_____

What did I do for others? _____

_____

_____

*What could I have done better?*_____

_____

_____

*What did I do well?*_____

_____

_____

Freedom from Bondage: Refer to the "Self Will * God's Will" chart and the "Freedom from Bondage" reading on the last pages of this journal.

God grant me freedom from _____ *and replace it with* _____
God grant me freedom from _____ *and replace it with* _____
God grant me freedom from _____ *and replace it with* _____
God grant me freedom from _____ *and replace it with* _____

*God, I pray for the health, prosperity, happiness and well-being of*_____
All the things I pray for myself, I pray also for _____

Review Eleventh Step Prayer on the last page of journal.

Morning Review:
(Review prayers from first page).

Plan of Eating: *Today, extra food is not an option.*

Water: ☐☐☐☐☐☐☐

Breakfast:_____
_____
_____

Lunch: _____
_____
_____

Dinner: _____
_____
_____

Snack:_____
_____
_____

Gratitudes: *(A grateful heart doesn't need to eat compulsively)* *Today, I thank God for:*
_____
_____
_____
_____
_____
_____

Something I like about myself:
_____
_____
_____
_____

Something to keep in mind today:
_____
_____
_____
_____

Daily Writing: Source: _____ Pages: _____
_____
_____
_____
_____
_____
_____
_____
_____
_____
_____
_____
_____
_____

Su M Tu W Th F Sat   *Date:* _____ *Day #:*_____

Evening Review: *(or anytime the need arises)*

Today was I:

   Resentful? _____

_____

   Selfish? _____

_____

   Dishonest? _____

_____

   Jealous? _____

_____

   Fearful: (Of losing something? Of not getting what I want? Of being found out?)

_____

_____

   *Restless, irritable or discontented?*_____

_____

Was I kind and loving towards all? _____

_____

_____

*Do I owe an apology?*_____

_____

_____

What did I do for others? _____

_____

_____

*What could I have done better?*_____

_____

_____

*What did I do well?*_____

_____

_____

Freedom from Bondage: Refer to the "Self Will * God's Will" chart and the "Freedom from Bondage" reading on the last pages of this journal.

God grant me freedom from _____ *and replace it with* _____
God grant me freedom from _____ *and replace it with* _____
God grant me freedom from _____ *and replace it with* _____
God grant me freedom from _____ *and replace it with* _____

*God, I pray for the health, prosperity, happiness and well-being of*_____
All the things I pray for myself, I pray also for _____

Review Eleventh Step Prayer on the last page of journal.

Morning Review:
(Review prayers from first page).

Plan of Eating: *Today, extra food is not an option.*

Water: ☐☐☐☐☐☐☐☐

Breakfast:_____
_____
_____

Lunch: _____
_____
_____

Dinner: _____
_____
_____

Snack:_____
_____
_____

Gratitudes: *(A grateful heart doesn't need to eat compulsively)*
Today, I thank God for:

_____
_____
_____
_____
_____
_____

Something I like about myself:

_____
_____
_____
_____
_____

Something to keep in mind today:

_____
_____
_____
_____
_____

Daily Writing: Source: _____ Pages: _____

_____
_____
_____
_____
_____
_____
_____
_____
_____
_____
_____
_____
_____
_____
_____

Su   M   Tu   W   Th   F   Sat   Date: _____   Day #:_____

Evening Review: *(or anytime the need arises)*

Today was I:

Resentful?   _____

_____

Selfish?   _____

_____

Dishonest?   _____

_____

Jealous?   _____

_____

Fearful: *(Of losing something? Of not getting what I want? Of being found out?)*

_____

_____

Restless, irritable or discontented?_____

_____

Was I kind and loving towards all? _____

_____

_____

Do I owe an apology?_____

_____

_____

What did I do for others? _____

_____

_____

What could I have done better?_____

_____

_____

What did I do well?_____

_____

_____

Freedom from Bondage: Refer to the "Self Will * God's Will" chart and the "Freedom from Bondage" reading on the last pages of this journal.

God grant me freedom from _____ *and replace it with* _____
God grant me freedom from _____ *and replace it with* _____
God grant me freedom from _____ *and replace it with* _____
God grant me freedom from _____ *and replace it with* _____

*God, I pray for the health, prosperity, happiness and well-being of*_____
All the things I pray for myself, I pray also for _____

Review Eleventh Step Prayer on the last page of journal.

Morning Review:
(*Review prayers from first page*).

Plan of Eating: *Today, extra food is not an option.*

Water: ☐☐☐☐☐☐☐

Breakfast:_____
_____
_____

Lunch: _____
_____
_____

Dinner: _____
_____
_____

Snack:_____
_____
_____

Gratitudes: (*A grateful heart doesn't need to eat compulsively*)
Today, I thank God for:

_____
_____
_____
_____
_____
_____

Something I like about myself:

_____
_____
_____
_____
_____

Something to keep in mind today:

_____
_____
_____
_____
_____

Daily Writing: Source: _____ Pages: _____

_____
_____
_____
_____
_____
_____
_____
_____
_____
_____
_____
_____
_____
_____

Su M Tu W Th F Sat   Date: _____ Day #:_____

Evening Review: *(or anytime the need arises)*

Today was I:

   Resentful?   _____

                      _____

   Selfish?   _____

                      _____

   Dishonest?   _____

                      _____

   Jealous?   _____

                      _____

   Fearful: (Of losing something? Of not getting what I want? Of being found out?)

                      _____

                      _____

   *Restless, irritable or discontented?*_____

                      _____

Was I kind and loving towards all? _____

_____

_____

*Do I owe an apology?*_____

_____

_____

What did I do for others? _____

_____

_____

*What could I have done better?*_____

_____

_____

*What did I do well?*_____

_____

_____

Freedom from Bondage: Refer to the "Self Will * God's Will" chart and the "Freedom from Bondage" reading on the last pages of this journal.

God grant me freedom from _____ *and replace it with* _____
God grant me freedom from _____ *and replace it with* _____
God grant me freedom from _____ *and replace it with* _____
God grant me freedom from _____ *and replace it with* _____

*God, I pray for the health, prosperity, happiness and well-being of*_____
All the things I pray for myself, I pray also for _____

Review Eleventh Step Prayer on the last page of journal.

Morning Review:

(Review prayers from first page).

Plan of Eating: *Today, extra food is not an option.*

Water: ☐☐☐☐☐☐☐☐

Breakfast:_____
_____
_____

Lunch: _____
_____
_____

Dinner: _____
_____
_____

Snack:_____
_____
_____

Gratitudes: *(A grateful heart doesn't need to eat compulsively)*
Today, I thank God for:

_____
_____
_____
_____
_____
_____

Something I like about myself:

_____
_____
_____
_____

Something to keep in mind today:

_____
_____
_____
_____

Daily Writing: Source: _____ Pages: _____

_____
_____
_____
_____
_____
_____
_____
_____
_____
_____
_____
_____
_____
_____
_____

Evening Review: *(or anytime the need arises)*

Today was I:

   Resentful? _____

   _____

   Selfish? _____

   _____

   Dishonest? _____

   _____

   Jealous? _____

   _____

   Fearful: (Of losing something? Of not getting what I want? Of being found out?)

   _____

   _____

   *Restless, irritable or discontented?*_____

   _____

Was I kind and loving towards all? _____

_____

*Do I owe an apology?*_____

_____

What did I do for others? _____

_____

*What could I have done better?*_____

_____

*What did I do well?*_____

_____

_____

Freedom from Bondage: Refer to the "Self Will * God's Will" chart and the "Freedom from Bondage" reading on the last pages of this journal.

God grant me freedom from _____ *and replace it with* _____
God grant me freedom from _____ *and replace it with* _____
God grant me freedom from _____ *and replace it with* _____
God grant me freedom from _____ *and replace it with* _____

*God, I pray for the health, prosperity, happiness and well-being of*_____
All the things I pray for myself, I pray also for _____

Review Eleventh Step Prayer on the last page of journal.

Morning Review:

(*Review prayers from first page*).

Plan of Eating: *Today, extra food is not an option.*

Water: ☐☐☐☐☐☐☐

Breakfast:_____

_____

_____

Lunch: _____

_____

_____

Dinner: _____

_____

_____

Snack:_____

_____

_____

Gratitudes: (*A grateful heart doesn't need to eat compulsively*) *Today, I thank God for*:

_____

_____

_____

_____

_____

_____

Something I like about myself:

_____

_____

_____

_____

_____

Something to keep in mind today:

_____

_____

_____

_____

_____

Daily Writing: Source: _____ Pages: _____

_____

_____

_____

_____

_____

_____

_____

_____

_____

_____

_____

_____

_____

_____

_____

Su M Tu W Th F Sat   Date: _____ Day #:_____

Evening Review: *(or anytime the need arises)*

Today was I:

   Resentful?   _____

                    _____

   Selfish?   _____

                    _____

   Dishonest?   _____

                    _____

   Jealous?   _____

                    _____

   Fearful: (Of losing something? Of not getting what I want? Of being found out?)

                    _____

                    _____

   *Restless, irritable or discontented?*_____

                    _____

Was I kind and loving towards all? _____

_____

_____

*Do I owe an apology?*_____

_____

What did I do for others? _____

_____

*What could I have done better?*_____

_____

_____

*What did I do well?*_____

_____

_____

Freedom from Bondage: Refer to the "Self Will * God's Will" chart and the "Freedom from Bondage" reading on the last pages of this journal.

God grant me freedom from   _____ *and replace it with* _____
God grant me freedom from   _____ *and replace it with* _____
God grant me freedom from   _____ *and replace it with* _____
God grant me freedom from   _____ *and replace it with* _____

*God, I pray for the health, prosperity, happiness and well-being of*_____
All the things I pray for myself, I pray also for _____

Review Eleventh Step Prayer on the last page of journal.

Morning Review:
(Review prayers from first page).

Plan of Eating: *Today, extra food is not an option.*

Water: □□□□□□□

Breakfast:_____
_____
_____

Lunch: _____
_____
_____

Dinner: _____
_____
_____

Snack:_____
_____
_____

Gratitudes: *(A grateful heart doesn't need to eat compulsively)*
Today, I thank God for:

_____
_____
_____
_____
_____
_____

Something I like about myself:

_____
_____
_____
_____
_____

Something to keep in mind today:

_____
_____
_____
_____
_____

Daily Writing: Source: _____ Pages: _____

_____
_____
_____
_____
_____
_____
_____
_____
_____
_____
_____
_____
_____
_____

Su   M   Tu   W   Th   F   Sat   Date: _____ Day #:_____

Evening Review: *(or anytime the need arises)*

Today was I:

   Resentful?   _____

                   _____

   Selfish?   _____

                   _____

   Dishonest?   _____

                   _____

   Jealous?   _____

                   _____

   Fearful: (Of losing something? Of not getting what I want? Of being found out?)

                   _____

                   _____

   *Restless, irritable or discontented?*_____

                   _____

Was I kind and loving towards all? _____

_____

Do I owe an apology? _____

_____

What did I do for others? _____

_____

*What could I have done better?*_____

_____

*What did I do well?*_____

_____

_____

Freedom from Bondage: Refer to the "Self Will * God's Will" chart and the "Freedom from Bondage" reading on the last pages of this journal.

God grant me freedom from _____ *and replace it with* _____

God grant me freedom from _____ *and replace it with* _____

God grant me freedom from _____ *and replace it with* _____

God grant me freedom from _____ *and replace it with* _____

*God, I pray for the health, prosperity, happiness and well-being of*_____

All the things I pray for myself, I pray also for _____

Review Eleventh Step Prayer on the last page of journal.

Morning Review:

(Review prayers from first page).

Plan of Eating: *Today, extra food is not an option.*

Water: ☐☐☐☐☐☐☐

Breakfast:_____
_____
_____

Lunch: _____
_____
_____

Dinner: _____
_____
_____

Snack:_____
_____
_____

Gratitudes: *(A grateful heart doesn't need to eat compulsively)* *Today, I thank God for:*

_____
_____
_____
_____
_____
_____

Something I like about myself:

_____
_____
_____
_____
_____

Something to keep in mind today:

_____
_____
_____
_____
_____

Daily Writing: Source: _____ Pages: _____

_____
_____
_____
_____
_____
_____
_____
_____
_____
_____
_____
_____
_____
_____
_____

Su   M   Tu   W   Th   F   Sat   Date: _____ Day #:_____

Evening Review: *(or anytime the need arises)*

Today was I:

    Resentful? _____

_____

    Selfish? _____

_____

    Dishonest? _____

_____

    Jealous? _____

_____

    Fearful: (Of losing something? Of not getting what I want? Of being found out?)

_____

_____

    *Restless, irritable or discontented?*_____

_____

Was I kind and loving towards all? _____

_____

*Do I owe an apology?*_____

_____

What did I do for others? _____

_____

*What could I have done better?*_____

_____

*What did I do well?*_____

_____

Freedom from Bondage: Refer to the "Self Will * God's Will" chart and the "Freedom from Bondage" reading on the last pages of this journal.

God grant me freedom from _____ *and replace it with* _____
God grant me freedom from _____ *and replace it with* _____
God grant me freedom from _____ *and replace it with* _____
God grant me freedom from _____ *and replace it with* _____

*God, I pray for the health, prosperity, happiness and well-being of*_____
All the things I pray for myself, I pray also for _____

Review Eleventh Step Prayer on the last page of journal.

Morning Review:

(Review prayers from first page).

Plan of Eating: *Today, extra food is not an option.*

Water: ☐☐☐☐☐☐☐

Breakfast:_____

_____

_____

Lunch: _____

_____

_____

Dinner: _____

_____

_____

Snack:_____

_____

_____

Gratitudes: *(A grateful heart doesn't need to eat compulsively)* *Today, I thank God for:*

_____

_____

_____

_____

_____

_____

Something I like about myself:

_____

_____

_____

_____

_____

Something to keep in mind today:

_____

_____

_____

_____

_____

Daily Writing: Source: _____ Pages: _____

_____

_____

_____

_____

_____

_____

_____

_____

_____

_____

_____

_____

_____

_____

Evening Review: *(or anytime the need arises)*

Today was I:

   Resentful? _____

_____

   Selfish? _____

_____

   Dishonest? _____

_____

   Jealous? _____

_____

   Fearful: (Of losing something? Of not getting what I want? Of being found out?)

_____

_____

   Restless, irritable or discontented? _____

_____

Was I kind and loving towards all? _____

_____

Do I owe an apology? _____

_____

What did I do for others? _____

_____

What could I have done better? _____

_____

What did I do well? _____

_____

_____

Freedom from Bondage: Refer to the "Self Will * God's Will" chart and the "Freedom from Bondage" reading on the last pages of this journal.

God grant me freedom from _____ *and replace it with* _____
God grant me freedom from _____ *and replace it with* _____
God grant me freedom from _____ *and replace it with* _____
God grant me freedom from _____ *and replace it with* _____

God, I pray for the health, prosperity, happiness and well-being of _____
All the things I pray for myself, I pray also for _____

Review Eleventh Step Prayer on the last page of journal.

Morning Review:
(Review prayers from first page).

Plan of Eating: *Today, extra food is not an option.*

Water: ☐☐☐☐☐☐☐

Breakfast:_____
_____
_____

Lunch: _____
_____
_____

Dinner: _____
_____
_____

Snack:_____
_____
_____

Gratitudes: (*A grateful heart doesn't need to eat compulsively*) *Today, I thank God for:*

_____
_____
_____
_____
_____
_____

Something I like about myself:

_____
_____
_____
_____
_____

Something to keep in mind today:

_____
_____
_____
_____
_____

Daily Writing: Source: _____ Pages: _____

_____
_____
_____
_____
_____
_____
_____
_____
_____
_____
_____
_____
_____
_____
_____

Su   M   Tu   W   Th   F   Sat   Date:_____ Day #:_____

Evening Review: *(or anytime the need arises)*

Today was I:

   Resentful?   _____

                       _____

   Selfish?   _____

                       _____

   Dishonest?   _____

                       _____

   Jealous?   _____

                       _____

   Fearful: (Of losing something? Of not getting what I want? Of being found out?)

                       _____

                       _____

   *Restless, irritable or discontented?*_____

                       _____

Was I kind and loving towards all? _____

_____

_____

*Do I owe an apology?*_____

_____

_____

What did I do for others? _____

_____

_____

*What could I have done better?*_____

_____

_____

*What did I do well?*_____

_____

_____

Freedom from Bondage: Refer to the "Self Will * God's Will" chart and the "Freedom from Bondage" reading on the last pages of this journal.

God grant me freedom from _____ *and replace it with* _____
God grant me freedom from _____ *and replace it with* _____
God grant me freedom from _____ *and replace it with* _____
God grant me freedom from _____ *and replace it with* _____

*God, I pray for the health, prosperity, happiness and well-being of*_____
All the things I pray for myself, I pray also for _____

Review Eleventh Step Prayer on the last page of journal.

Morning Review:
(Review prayers from first page).

Plan of Eating: *Today, extra food is not an option.*

Water: ⬜⬜⬜⬜⬜⬜⬜

Breakfast:_____
_____
_____

Lunch: _____
_____
_____

Dinner: _____
_____
_____

Snack:_____
_____
_____

Gratitudes: (*A grateful heart doesn't need to eat compulsively*) *Today, I thank God for:*

_____
_____
_____
_____
_____
_____

Something I like about myself:

_____
_____
_____
_____
_____

Something to keep in mind today:

_____
_____
_____
_____

Daily Writing: Source: _____ Pages: _____

_____
_____
_____
_____
_____
_____
_____
_____
_____
_____
_____
_____
_____
_____
_____

Evening Review: *(or anytime the need arises)*

Today was I:

Resentful?   _____

_____

Selfish?   _____

_____

Dishonest?   _____

_____

Jealous?   _____

_____

Fearful: (Of losing something? Of not getting what I want? Of being found out?)

_____

_____

Restless, irritable or discontented?_____

_____

Was I kind and loving towards all? _____

_____

Do I owe an apology? _____

_____

What did I do for others? _____

_____

What could I have done better?_____

_____

What did I do well?_____

_____

Freedom from Bondage: Refer to the "Self Will * God's Will" chart and the "Freedom from Bondage" reading on the last pages of this journal.

God grant me freedom from _____ *and replace it with* _____
God grant me freedom from _____ *and replace it with* _____
God grant me freedom from _____ *and replace it with* _____
God grant me freedom from _____ *and replace it with* _____

*God, I pray for the health, prosperity, happiness and well-being of*_____
All the things I pray for myself, I pray also for _____

Review Eleventh Step Prayer on the last page of journal.

Morning Review:

(Review prayers from first page).

Plan of Eating: *Today, extra food is not an option.*

Water: ☐☐☐☐☐☐☐

Breakfast:_____
_____
_____

Lunch: _____
_____
_____

Dinner: _____
_____
_____

Snack:_____
_____
_____

Gratitudes: *(A grateful heart doesn't need to eat compulsively)*
Today, I thank God for:

_____
_____
_____
_____
_____
_____

Something I like about myself:

_____
_____
_____
_____
_____

Something to keep in mind today:

_____
_____
_____
_____

Daily Writing: Source: _____ Pages: _____

_____
_____
_____
_____
_____
_____
_____
_____
_____
_____
_____
_____
_____
_____

Su   M   Tu   W   Th   F   Sat   Date: _____ Day #:_____

Evening Review: *(or anytime the need arises)*

Today was I:

   Resentful? _____

   _____

   Selfish? _____

   _____

   Dishonest? _____

   _____

   Jealous? _____

   _____

   Fearful: (Of losing something? Of not getting what I want? Of being found out?)

   _____

   _____

   Restless, irritable or discontented? _____

   _____

Was I kind and loving towards all? _____

_____

_____

Do I owe an apology? _____

_____

_____

What did I do for others? _____

_____

_____

What could I have done better? _____

_____

_____

What did I do well? _____

_____

_____

Freedom from Bondage: Refer to the "Self Will * God's Will" chart and the "Freedom from Bondage" reading on the last pages of this journal.

God grant me freedom from _____ *and replace it with* _____
God grant me freedom from _____ *and replace it with* _____
God grant me freedom from _____ *and replace it with* _____
God grant me freedom from _____ *and replace it with* _____

God, I pray for the health, prosperity, happiness and well-being of _____
All the things I pray for myself, I pray also for _____

Review Eleventh Step Prayer on the last page of journal.

Morning Review:
(Review prayers from first page).

Plan of Eating: *Today, extra food is not an option.*

Water: ☐☐☐☐☐☐☐

Breakfast:_____
_____
_____

Lunch: _____
_____
_____

Dinner: _____
_____
_____

Snack:_____
_____
_____

Gratitudes: (*A grateful heart doesn't need to eat compulsively*) *Today, I thank God for*:

_____
_____
_____
_____
_____
_____

Something I like about myself:

_____
_____
_____
_____
_____

Something to keep in mind today:

_____
_____
_____
_____
_____

Daily Writing: Source: _____ Pages: _____

_____
_____
_____
_____
_____
_____
_____
_____
_____
_____
_____
_____
_____
_____

Evening Review: *(or anytime the need arises)*

Today was I:

    Resentful?   _____

                       _____

    Selfish?   _____

                       _____

    Dishonest?   _____

                       _____

    Jealous?   _____

                       _____

    Fearful: (Of losing something? Of not getting what I want? Of being found out?)

                       _____

                       _____

    *Restless, irritable or discontented?*_____

                       _____

Was I kind and loving towards all? _____

_____

*Do I owe an apology?*_____

_____

What did I do for others? _____

_____

*What could I have done better?*_____

_____

_____

*What did I do well?*_____

_____

_____

Freedom from Bondage: Refer to the "Self Will * God's Will" chart and the "Freedom from Bondage" reading on the last pages of this journal.

God grant me freedom from _____ *and replace it with*_____
God grant me freedom from _____ *and replace it with*_____
God grant me freedom from _____ *and replace it with*_____
God grant me freedom from _____ *and replace it with*_____

*God, I pray for the health, prosperity, happiness and well-being of*_____
All the things I pray for myself, I pray also for _____

Review Eleventh Step Prayer on the last page of journal.

Morning Review:
(*Review prayers from first page*).

Plan of Eating: *Today, extra food is not an option.*

Water: ☐☐☐☐☐☐☐

Breakfast:_____
_____
_____

Lunch: _____
_____
_____

Dinner:_____
_____
_____

Snack:_____
_____
_____

Gratitudes: (*A grateful heart doesn't need to eat compulsively*) *Today, I thank God for*:

_____
_____
_____
_____
_____
_____

Something I like about myself:

_____
_____
_____
_____

Something to keep in mind today:

_____
_____
_____
_____

Daily Writing: Source: _____ Pages: _____

_____
_____
_____
_____
_____
_____
_____
_____
_____
_____
_____
_____
_____
_____

Su   M   Tu   W   Th   F   Sat   Date: _____ Day #:_____

Evening Review: *(or anytime the need arises)*

Today was I:

   Resentful? _____

                _____

   Selfish? _____

                _____

   Dishonest? _____

                _____

   Jealous? _____

                _____

   Fearful: *(Of losing something? Of not getting what I want? Of being found out?)*

                _____

                _____

   Restless, irritable or discontented?_____

                _____

Was I kind and loving towards all? _____

_____

*Do I owe an apology?*_____

_____

What did I do for others? _____

_____

*What could I have done better?*_____

_____

*What did I do well?*_____

_____

_____

Freedom from Bondage: Refer to the "Self Will * God's Will" chart and the "Freedom from Bondage" reading on the last pages of this journal.

God grant me freedom from _____ *and replace it with* _____
God grant me freedom from _____ *and replace it with* _____
God grant me freedom from _____ *and replace it with* _____
God grant me freedom from _____ *and replace it with* _____

*God, I pray for the health, prosperity, happiness and well-being of*_____
All the things I pray for myself, I pray also for _____

Review Eleventh Step Prayer on the last page of journal.

Morning Review:
(*Review prayers from first page*).

Plan of Eating: *Today, extra food is not an option.*

Water: ☐☐☐☐☐☐☐

Breakfast:_____
_____
_____

Lunch: _____
_____
_____

Dinner: _____
_____
_____

Snack:_____
_____
_____

Gratitudes: (*A grateful heart doesn't need to eat compulsively*) *Today, I thank God for*:

_____
_____
_____
_____
_____
_____

Something I like about myself:

_____
_____
_____
_____
_____

Something to keep in mind today:

_____
_____
_____
_____
_____

Daily Writing: Source: _____ Pages: _____

_____
_____
_____
_____
_____
_____
_____
_____
_____
_____
_____
_____
_____
_____
_____

Su   M   Tu   W   Th   F   Sat   Date: _____ Day #:_____

Evening Review: *(or anytime the need arises)*

Today was I:

   Resentful?   _____

   _____

   Selfish?   _____

   _____

   Dishonest?   _____

   _____

   Jealous?   _____

   _____

   Fearful: (Of losing something? Of not getting what I want? Of being found out?)

   _____

   _____

   Restless, irritable or discontented?_____

   _____

Was I kind and loving towards all? _____

_____

_____

*Do I owe an apology?*_____

_____

_____

What did I do for others? _____

_____

_____

*What could I have done better?*_____

_____

_____

*What did I do well?*_____

_____

_____

Freedom from Bondage: Refer to the "Self Will * God's Will" chart and the "Freedom from Bondage" reading on the last pages of this journal.

God grant me freedom from _____ *and replace it with* _____
God grant me freedom from _____ *and replace it with* _____
God grant me freedom from _____ *and replace it with* _____
God grant me freedom from _____ *and replace it with* _____

*God, I pray for the health, prosperity, happiness and well-being of*_____
All the things I pray for myself, I pray also for _____

Review Eleventh Step Prayer on the last page of journal.

Morning Review:
(Review prayers from first page).

Plan of Eating: *Today, extra food is not an option.*

Water: □□□□□□□

Breakfast:_____
_____
_____

Lunch: _____
_____
_____

Dinner: _____
_____
_____

Snack:_____
_____
_____

Gratitudes: (*A grateful heart doesn't need to eat compulsively*) *Today, I thank God for*:

_____
_____
_____
_____
_____
_____

Something I like about myself:

_____
_____
_____
_____
_____

Something to keep in mind today:

_____
_____
_____
_____
_____

Daily Writing: Source: _____ Pages: _____

_____
_____
_____
_____
_____
_____
_____
_____
_____
_____
_____
_____
_____
_____

Su M Tu W Th F Sat   *Date:* _____ *Day #:*_____

Evening Review: *(or anytime the need arises)*

Today was I:

    Resentful? _____

    _____

    Selfish? _____

    _____

    Dishonest? _____

    _____

    Jealous? _____

    _____

    Fearful: (Of losing something? Of not getting what I want? Of being found out?)

    _____

    _____

    *Restless, irritable or discontented?*_____

    _____

Was I kind and loving towards all? _____

_____

_____

Do I owe an apology? _____

_____

_____

What did I do for others? _____

_____

_____

*What could I have done better?*_____

_____

_____

*What did I do well?*_____

_____

_____

Freedom from Bondage: Refer to the "Self Will * God's Will" chart and the "Freedom from Bondage" reading on the last pages of this journal.

God grant me freedom from _____ *and replace it with* _____
God grant me freedom from _____ *and replace it with* _____
God grant me freedom from _____ *and replace it with* _____
God grant me freedom from _____ *and replace it with* _____

*God, I pray for the health, prosperity, happiness and well-being of*_____
All the things I pray for myself, I pray also for _____

Review Eleventh Step Prayer on the last page of journal.

Morning Review:
(Review prayers from first page).

Plan of Eating: *Today, extra food is not an option.*

Water: ☐☐☐☐☐☐☐

Breakfast:_____
_____
_____

Lunch: _____
_____
_____

Dinner: _____
_____
_____

Snack:_____
_____
_____

Gratitudes: *(A grateful heart doesn't need to eat compulsively)* *Today, I thank God for:*

_____
_____
_____
_____
_____
_____

Something I like about myself:

_____
_____
_____
_____

Something to keep in mind today:

_____
_____
_____
_____

Daily Writing: Source: _____ Pages: _____

_____
_____
_____
_____
_____
_____
_____
_____
_____
_____
_____
_____
_____
_____
_____

Su   M   Tu   W   Th   F   Sat   Date: _____ Day #:_____

Evening Review: *(or anytime the need arises)*

Today was I:

   Resentful? _____

   _____

   Selfish? _____

   _____

   Dishonest? _____

   _____

   Jealous? _____

   _____

   Fearful: (Of losing something? Of not getting what I want? Of being found out?)

   _____

   _____

   *Restless, irritable or discontented?*_____

   _____

Was I kind and loving towards all? _____

_____

_____

*Do I owe an apology?*_____

_____

_____

What did I do for others? _____

_____

_____

*What could I have done better?*_____

_____

_____

*What did I do well?*_____

_____

_____

Freedom from Bondage: Refer to the "Self Will * God's Will" chart and the "Freedom from Bondage" reading on the last pages of this journal.

God grant me freedom from _____ *and replace it with* _____
God grant me freedom from _____ *and replace it with* _____
God grant me freedom from _____ *and replace it with* _____
God grant me freedom from _____ *and replace it with* _____

*God, I pray for the health, prosperity, happiness and well-being of*_____
All the things I pray for myself, I pray also for _____

Review Eleventh Step Prayer on the last page of journal.

Morning Review:
(Review prayers from first page).

Plan of Eating: *Today, extra food is not an option.*

Water: ☐☐☐☐☐☐☐☐

Breakfast:_____
_____
_____

Lunch: _____
_____
_____

Dinner: _____
_____
_____

Snack:_____
_____
_____

Gratitudes: *(A grateful heart doesn't need to eat compulsively)* *Today, I thank God for:*

_____
_____
_____
_____
_____
_____

Something I like about myself:

_____
_____
_____
_____
_____

Something to keep in mind today:

_____
_____
_____
_____

Daily Writing: Source: _____ Pages: _____

_____
_____
_____
_____
_____
_____
_____
_____
_____
_____
_____
_____
_____
_____

Su   M   Tu   W   Th   F   Sat   Date: _____ Day #:_____

Evening Review: *(or anytime the need arises)*

Today was I:

   Resentful?   _____

                                      _____

   Selfish?   _____

                                        _____

   Dishonest?   _____

                                        _____

   Jealous?   _____

   Fearful: (Of losing something? Of not getting what I want? Of being found out?)

                                        _____

                                        _____

   *Restless, irritable or discontented?*_____

                                        _____

Was I kind and loving towards all? _____

_____

_____

*Do I owe an apology?*_____

_____

_____

What did I do for others? _____

_____

_____

*What could I have done better?*_____

_____

_____

*What did I do well?*_____

_____

_____

Freedom from Bondage: Refer to the "Self Will * God's Will" chart and the "Freedom from Bondage" reading on the last pages of this journal.

God grant me freedom from _____ *and replace it with* _____
God grant me freedom from _____ *and replace it with* _____
God grant me freedom from _____ *and replace it with* _____
God grant me freedom from _____ *and replace it with* _____

*God, I pray for the health, prosperity, happiness and well-being of*_____
All the things I pray for myself, I pray also for _____

Review Eleventh Step Prayer on the last page of journal.

Morning Review:
(Review prayers from first page).

Plan of Eating: *Today, extra food is not an option.*

Water: ☐☐☐☐☐☐☐

Breakfast:_____
_____
_____

Lunch: _____
_____
_____

Dinner: _____
_____
_____

Snack:_____
_____
_____

Gratitudes: *(A grateful heart doesn't need to eat compulsively)* Today, I thank God for:

_____
_____
_____
_____
_____
_____

Something I like about myself:

_____
_____
_____
_____
_____

Something to keep in mind today:

_____
_____
_____
_____

Daily Writing: Source: _____ Pages: _____

_____
_____
_____
_____
_____
_____
_____
_____
_____
_____
_____
_____
_____
_____

Su   M   Tu   W   Th   F   Sat   Date: _____ Day #:_____

Evening Review: *(or anytime the need arises)*

Today was I:

   Resentful?   _____

   _____

   Selfish?   _____

   _____

   Dishonest?   _____

   _____

   Jealous?   _____

   _____

   Fearful: (Of losing something? Of not getting what I want? Of being found out?)

   _____

   _____

   *Restless, irritable or discontented?*_____

   _____

Was I kind and loving towards all? _____

_____

_____

*Do I owe an apology?*_____

_____

_____

What did I do for others? _____

_____

_____

*What could I have done better?*_____

_____

_____

*What did I do well?*_____

_____

_____

Freedom from Bondage: Refer to the "Self Will * God's Will" chart and the "Freedom from Bondage" reading on the last pages of this journal.

God grant me freedom from _____ *and replace it with* _____
God grant me freedom from _____ *and replace it with* _____
God grant me freedom from _____ *and replace it with* _____
God grant me freedom from _____ *and replace it with* _____

*God, I pray for the health, prosperity, happiness and well-being of*_____
All the things I pray for myself, I pray also for _____

Review Eleventh Step Prayer on the last page of journal.

Morning Review:

(Review prayers from first page).

Plan of Eating: *Today, extra food is not an option.*

Water: ☐☐☐☐☐☐☐

Breakfast:_____
_____
_____

Lunch: _____
_____
_____

Dinner:_____
_____
_____

Snack:_____
_____
_____

Gratitudes: *(A grateful heart doesn't need to eat compulsively)* Today, I thank God for:

_____
_____
_____
_____
_____
_____

Something I like about myself:

_____
_____
_____
_____
_____

Something to keep in mind today:

_____
_____
_____
_____
_____

Daily Writing: Source: _____ Pages: _____

_____
_____
_____
_____
_____
_____
_____
_____
_____
_____
_____
_____
_____
_____
_____

Su   M   Tu   W   Th   F   Sat   Date: _____ Day #:_____

Evening Review: *(or anytime the need arises)*

Today was I:

   Resentful?   _____

                   _____

   Selfish?   _____

                   _____

   Dishonest?   _____

                   _____

   Jealous?   _____

                   _____

   Fearful: (Of losing something? Of not getting what I want? Of being found out?)

                   _____

                   _____

   *Restless, irritable or discontented?*_____

                   _____

Was I kind and loving towards all? _____

_____

*Do I owe an apology?*_____

_____

What did I do for others? _____

_____

*What could I have done better?*_____

_____

*What did I do well?*_____

_____

_____

Freedom from Bondage: Refer to the "Self Will * God's Will" chart and the "Freedom from Bondage" reading on the last pages of this journal.

God grant me freedom from _____ *and replace it with* _____
God grant me freedom from _____ *and replace it with* _____
God grant me freedom from _____ *and replace it with* _____
God grant me freedom from _____ *and replace it with* _____

*God, I pray for the health, prosperity, happiness and well-being of*_____
All the things I pray for myself, I pray also for _____

Review Eleventh Step Prayer on the last page of journal.

Morning Review:

(Review prayers from first page).

Plan of Eating: *Today, extra food is not an option.*

Water: ☐☐☐☐☐☐☐

Breakfast:_____

_____

_____

Lunch: _____

_____

_____

Dinner: _____

_____

_____

Snack:_____

_____

_____

Gratitudes: *(A grateful heart doesn't need to eat compulsively)* Today, I thank God for:

_____

_____

_____

_____

_____

_____

Something I like about myself:

_____

_____

_____

_____

_____

Something to keep in mind today:

_____

_____

_____

_____

_____

Daily Writing: Source: _____ Pages: _____

_____

_____

_____

_____

_____

_____

_____

_____

_____

_____

_____

_____

_____

_____

Su   M   Tu   W   Th   F   Sat   Date: _____   Day #:_____

Evening Review: *(or anytime the need arises)*

Today was I:

Resentful?   _____

_____

Selfish?   _____

_____

Dishonest?   _____

_____

Jealous?   _____

_____

Fearful: (Of losing something? Of not getting what I want? Of being found out?)

_____

_____

*Restless, irritable or discontented?*_____

_____

Was I kind and loving towards all? _____

_____

_____

*Do I owe an apology?*_____

_____

_____

What did I do for others? _____

_____

_____

*What could I have done better?*_____

_____

_____

*What did I do well?*_____

_____

_____

Freedom from Bondage: Refer to the "Self Will * God's Will" chart and the "Freedom from Bondage" reading on the last pages of this journal.

God grant me freedom from _____ *and replace it with* _____

God grant me freedom from _____ *and replace it with* _____

God grant me freedom from _____ *and replace it with* _____

God grant me freedom from _____ *and replace it with* _____

*God, I pray for the health, prosperity, happiness and well-being of*_____

All the things I pray for myself, I pray also for _____

Review Eleventh Step Prayer on the last page of journal.

Morning Review:
(Review prayers from first page).

Plan of Eating: *Today, extra food is not an option.*

Water: ☐☐☐☐☐☐☐☐

Breakfast:_____
_____
_____

Lunch: _____
_____
_____

Dinner: _____
_____
_____

Snack:_____
_____
_____

Gratitudes: (*A grateful heart doesn't need to eat compulsively*) *Today, I thank God for*:

_____
_____
_____
_____
_____
_____

Something I like about myself:

_____
_____
_____
_____

Something to keep in mind today:

_____
_____
_____
_____

Daily Writing: Source: _____ Pages: _____
_____
_____
_____
_____
_____
_____
_____
_____
_____
_____
_____
_____
_____
_____

Su   M   Tu   W   Th   F   Sat   Date: _____ Day #:_____

Evening Review: *(or anytime the need arises)*

Today was I:

Resentful?   _____

_____

Selfish?   _____

_____

Dishonest?   _____

_____

Jealous?   _____

_____

Fearful: (Of losing something? Of not getting what I want? Of being found out?)

_____

_____

Restless, irritable or discontented?_____

_____

Was I kind and loving towards all? _____

_____

_____

Do I owe an apology?_____

_____

_____

What did I do for others? _____

_____

_____

What could I have done better?_____

_____

_____

What did I do well?_____

_____

_____

Freedom from Bondage: Refer to the "Self Will * God's Will" chart and the "Freedom from Bondage" reading on the last pages of this journal.

God grant me freedom from _____ *and replace it with* _____
God grant me freedom from _____ *and replace it with* _____
God grant me freedom from _____ *and replace it with* _____
God grant me freedom from _____ *and replace it with* _____

*God, I pray for the health, prosperity, happiness and well-being of*_____
All the things I pray for myself, I pray also for _____

Review Eleventh Step Prayer on the last page of journal.

Morning Review:
(Review prayers from first page).

Plan of Eating: *Today, extra food is not an option.*

Water: ☐☐☐☐☐☐☐

Breakfast:_____
_____
_____

Lunch: _____
_____
_____

Dinner: _____
_____
_____

Snack:_____
_____
_____

Gratitudes: *(A grateful heart doesn't need to eat compulsively)*
Today, I thank God for:
_____
_____
_____
_____
_____
_____

Something I like about myself:
_____
_____
_____
_____
_____

Something to keep in mind today:
_____
_____
_____
_____

Daily Writing: Source: _____ Pages: _____

_____
_____
_____
_____
_____
_____
_____
_____
_____
_____
_____
_____
_____
_____
_____

Evening Review: *(or anytime the need arises)*

Today was I:

    Resentful?   _____

_____

    Selfish?   _____

_____

    Dishonest?   _____

_____

    Jealous?   _____

_____

    Fearful: (Of losing something? Of not getting what I want? Of being found out?)

_____

_____

    *Restless, irritable or discontented?*_____

_____

Was I kind and loving towards all? _____

_____

*Do I owe an apology?*_____

_____

What did I do for others? _____

_____

*What could I have done better?*_____

_____

*What did I do well?*_____

_____

_____

Freedom from Bondage: Refer to the "Self Will * God's Will" chart and the "Freedom from Bondage" reading on the last pages of this journal.

God grant me freedom from _____ *and replace it with*_____
God grant me freedom from _____ *and replace it with*_____
God grant me freedom from _____ *and replace it with*_____
God grant me freedom from _____ *and replace it with*_____

*God, I pray for the health, prosperity, happiness and well-being of*_____
All the things I pray for myself, I pray also for _____

Review Eleventh Step Prayer on the last page of journal.

Morning Review:

(Review prayers from first page).

Plan of Eating: *Today, extra food is not an option.*

Water: ☐☐☐☐☐☐☐

Breakfast:_____

_____

_____

Lunch: _____

_____

_____

Dinner: _____

_____

_____

Snack:_____

_____

_____

Gratitudes: *(A grateful heart doesn't need to eat compulsively)*
Today, I thank God for:

_____

_____

_____

_____

_____

_____

Something I like about myself:

_____

_____

_____

_____

_____

Something to keep in mind today:

_____

_____

_____

_____

_____

Daily Writing: Source: _____ Pages: _____

_____

_____

_____

_____

_____

_____

_____

_____

_____

_____

_____

_____

_____

_____

_____

Su   M   Tu   W   Th   F   Sat   Date: _____ Day #:_____

Evening Review: *(or anytime the need arises)*

Today was I:

Resentful?   _____

_____

Selfish?   _____

_____

Dishonest?   _____

_____

Jealous?   _____

_____

Fearful: *(Of losing something? Of not getting what I want? Of being found out?)*

_____

_____

Restless, irritable or discontented?_____

_____

Was I kind and loving towards all? _____

_____

Do I owe an apology? _____

_____

What did I do for others? _____

_____

What could I have done better?_____

_____

What did I do well?_____

_____

_____

Freedom from Bondage: Refer to the "Self Will * God's Will" chart and the "Freedom from Bondage" reading on the last pages of this journal.

God grant me freedom from _____ *and replace it with*_____
God grant me freedom from _____ *and replace it with*_____
God grant me freedom from _____ *and replace it with*_____
God grant me freedom from _____ *and replace it with*_____

*God, I pray for the health, prosperity, happiness and well-being of*_____
All the things I pray for myself, I pray also for _____

Review Eleventh Step Prayer on the last page of journal.

Morning Review:
(*Review prayers from first page*).

Plan of Eating: *Today, extra food is not an option.*

Water: ☐☐☐☐☐☐☐☐

Breakfast:_____
_____
_____

Lunch: _____
_____
_____

Dinner: _____
_____
_____

Snack:_____
_____
_____

Gratitudes: (*A grateful heart doesn't need to eat compulsively*)
Today, I thank God for:

_____
_____
_____
_____
_____
_____

Something I like about myself:

_____
_____
_____
_____
_____

Something to keep in mind today:

_____
_____
_____
_____
_____

Daily Writing: Source: _____ Pages: _____

_____
_____
_____
_____
_____
_____
_____
_____
_____
_____
_____
_____
_____
_____

Su   M   Tu   W   Th   F   Sat   Date: _____ Day #:_____

Evening Review: *(or anytime the need arises)*

Today was I:

Resentful?   _____

                    _____

Selfish?   _____

                    _____

Dishonest?   _____

                    _____

Jealous?   _____

                    _____

Fearful: *(Of losing something? Of not getting what I want? Of being found out?)*

                    _____

                    _____

Restless, irritable or discontented?_____

                    _____

Was I kind and loving towards all? _____

_____

_____

Do I owe an apology?_____

_____

_____

What did I do for others? _____

_____

_____

What could I have done better?_____

_____

_____

What did I do well?_____

_____

_____

Freedom from Bondage: Refer to the "Self Will * God's Will" chart and the "Freedom from Bondage" reading on the last pages of this journal.

God grant me freedom from _____ *and replace it with* _____
God grant me freedom from _____ *and replace it with* _____
God grant me freedom from _____ *and replace it with* _____
God grant me freedom from _____ *and replace it with* _____

*God, I pray for the health, prosperity, happiness and well-being of*_____
All the things I pray for myself, I pray also for _____

Review Eleventh Step Prayer on the last page of journal.

Morning Review:

(Review prayers from first page).

Plan of Eating: *Today, extra food is not an option.*

Water: ☐☐☐☐☐☐☐

Breakfast:_____

_____

_____

Lunch: _____

_____

_____

Dinner: _____

_____

_____

Snack:_____

_____

_____

Gratitudes: *(A grateful heart doesn't need to eat compulsively) Today, I thank God for:*

_____

_____

_____

_____

_____

_____

Something I like about myself:

_____

_____

_____

_____

_____

Something to keep in mind today:

_____

_____

_____

_____

Daily Writing: Source: _____ Pages: _____

_____

_____

_____

_____

_____

_____

_____

_____

_____

_____

_____

_____

_____

_____

Su   M   Tu   W   Th   F   Sat   Date: _____ Day #:_____

Evening Review: *(or anytime the need arises)*

Today was I:

   Resentful?   _____
                         _____

   Selfish?   _____
                         _____

   Dishonest?   _____
                         _____

   Jealous?   _____
                         _____

   Fearful: (Of losing something? Of not getting what I want? Of being found out?)
                         _____
                         _____

   Restless, irritable or discontented?_____
                         _____

Was I kind and loving towards all? _____
_____
_____

Do I owe an apology?_____
_____
_____

What did I do for others? _____
_____
_____

What could I have done better?_____
_____
_____

What did I do well?_____
_____
_____

Freedom from Bondage: Refer to the "Self Will * God's Will" chart and the
"Freedom from Bondage" reading on the last pages of this journal.

God grant me freedom from _____ *and replace it with* _____
God grant me freedom from _____ *and replace it with* _____
God grant me freedom from _____ *and replace it with* _____
God grant me freedom from _____ *and replace it with* _____

God, I pray for the health, prosperity, happiness and well-being of_____
All the things I pray for myself, I pray also for _____

Review Eleventh Step Prayer on the last page of journal.

Morning Review:

(*Review prayers from first page*).

Plan of Eating: *Today, extra food is not an option.*

Water: ☐☐☐☐☐☐☐☐

Breakfast:_____

_____

_____

Lunch: _____

_____

_____

Dinner: _____

_____

_____

Snack:_____

_____

_____

Gratitudes: (*A grateful heart doesn't need to eat compulsively*) *Today, I thank God for*:

_____

_____

_____

_____

_____

_____

Something I like about myself:

_____

_____

_____

_____

_____

Something to keep in mind today:

_____

_____

_____

_____

_____

Daily Writing: Source: _____ Pages: _____

_____

_____

_____

_____

_____

_____

_____

_____

_____

_____

_____

_____

_____

_____

Evening Review: *(or anytime the need arises)*

Today was I:

   Resentful? _____

_____

   Selfish? _____

_____

   Dishonest? _____

_____

   Jealous? _____

_____

   Fearful: (Of losing something? Of not getting what I want? Of being found out?)

_____

_____

   *Restless, irritable or discontented?*_____

_____

Was I kind and loving towards all? _____

_____

_____

*Do I owe an apology?*_____

_____

_____

What did I do for others? _____

_____

_____

*What could I have done better?*_____

_____

_____

*What did I do well?*_____

_____

_____

Freedom from Bondage: Refer to the "Self Will * God's Will" chart and the "Freedom from Bondage" reading on the last pages of this journal.

God grant me freedom from _____ *and replace it with* _____

God grant me freedom from _____ *and replace it with* _____

God grant me freedom from _____ *and replace it with* _____

God grant me freedom from _____ *and replace it with* _____

*God, I pray for the health, prosperity, happiness and well-being of*_____

All the things I pray for myself, I pray also for _____

Review Eleventh Step Prayer on the last page of journal.

Morning Review:
(*Review prayers from first page*).

Plan of Eating: *Today, extra food is not an option.*

Water: ☐☐☐☐☐☐☐

Breakfast:_____

_____

_____

Lunch: _____

_____

_____

Dinner: _____

_____

_____

Snack:_____

_____

_____

Gratitudes: (*A grateful heart doesn't need to eat compulsively*) Today, I thank God for:

_____

_____

_____

_____

_____

_____

Something I like about myself:

_____

_____

_____

_____

_____

Something to keep in mind today:

_____

_____

_____

_____

Daily Writing: Source: _____ Pages: _____

_____

_____

_____

_____

_____

_____

_____

_____

_____

_____

_____

_____

_____

_____

Su   M   Tu   W   Th   F   Sat   Date: _____ Day #:_____

Evening Review: *(or anytime the need arises)*

Today was I:

    Resentful? _____

    _____

    Selfish? _____

    _____

    Dishonest? _____

    _____

    Jealous? _____

    _____

    Fearful: (Of losing something? Of not getting what I want? Of being found out?)

    _____

    _____

    Restless, irritable or discontented? _____

    _____

Was I kind and loving towards all? _____

_____

Do I owe an apology? _____

_____

What did I do for others? _____

_____

What could I have done better? _____

_____

What did I do well? _____

_____

_____

Freedom from Bondage: Refer to the "Self Will * God's Will" chart and the "Freedom from Bondage" reading on the last pages of this journal.

God grant me freedom from _____ *and replace it with* _____
God grant me freedom from _____ *and replace it with* _____
God grant me freedom from _____ *and replace it with* _____
God grant me freedom from _____ *and replace it with* _____

God, I pray for the health, prosperity, happiness and well-being of _____
All the things I pray for myself, I pray also for _____

Review Eleventh Step Prayer on the last page of journal.

Morning Review:
(Review prayers from first page).

Plan of Eating: *Today, extra food is not an option.*

Water: ☐☐☐☐☐☐☐

Breakfast:_____
_____
_____

Lunch: _____
_____
_____

Dinner: _____
_____
_____

Snack:_____
_____
_____

Gratitudes: (*A grateful heart doesn't need to eat compulsively*) *Today, I thank God for:*

_____
_____
_____
_____
_____
_____

Something I like about myself:

_____
_____
_____
_____
_____

Something to keep in mind today:

_____
_____
_____
_____

Daily Writing: Source: _____ Pages: _____

_____
_____
_____
_____
_____
_____
_____
_____
_____
_____
_____
_____
_____
_____

Su   M   Tu   W   Th   F   Sat   Date: _____   Day #:_____

Evening Review: *(or anytime the need arises)*

Today was I:

Resentful?   _____
          _____

Selfish?   _____
          _____

Dishonest?   _____
          _____

Jealous?   _____
          _____

Fearful: (Of losing something? Of not getting what I want? Of being found out?)
          _____
          _____

Restless, irritable or discontented?_____
          _____

Was I kind and loving towards all? _____
_____
_____

Do I owe an apology?_____
_____
_____

What did I do for others? _____
_____
_____

What could I have done better?_____
_____
_____

What did I do well?_____
_____
_____

Freedom from Bondage: Refer to the "Self Will * God's Will" chart and the
"Freedom from Bondage" reading on the last pages of this journal.

God grant me freedom from _____ *and replace it with* _____
God grant me freedom from _____ *and replace it with* _____
God grant me freedom from _____ *and replace it with* _____
God grant me freedom from _____ *and replace it with* _____

God, I pray for the health, prosperity, happiness and well-being of_____
All the things I pray for myself, I pray also for _____

Review Eleventh Step Prayer on the last page of journal.

Morning Review:

(Review prayers from first page).

Plan of Eating: *Today, extra food is not an option.*

Water: ☐☐☐☐☐☐☐

Breakfast:_____
_____
_____

Lunch: _____
_____
_____

Dinner: _____
_____
_____

Snack:_____
_____
_____

Gratitudes: *(A grateful heart doesn't need to eat compulsively)* *Today, I thank God for:*

_____
_____
_____
_____
_____

Something I like about myself:

_____
_____
_____
_____

Something to keep in mind today:

_____
_____
_____
_____

Daily Writing: Source: _____ Pages: _____

_____
_____
_____
_____
_____
_____
_____
_____
_____
_____
_____
_____
_____

Date: _____   Day #:_____

Evening Review: *(or anytime the need arises)*

Today was I:

   Resentful? _____

   _____

   Selfish? _____

   _____

   Dishonest? _____

   _____

   Jealous? _____

   _____

   Fearful: *(Of losing something? Of not getting what I want? Of being found out?)*

   _____

   _____

   Restless, irritable or discontented?_____

   _____

Was I kind and loving towards all? _____

_____

_____

Do I owe an apology? _____

_____

_____

What did I do for others? _____

_____

_____

*What could I have done better?*_____

_____

_____

*What did I do well?*_____

_____

_____

Freedom from Bondage: Refer to the "Self Will * God's Will" chart and the "Freedom from Bondage" reading on the last pages of this journal.

God grant me freedom from _____ *and replace it with* _____
God grant me freedom from _____ *and replace it with* _____
God grant me freedom from _____ *and replace it with* _____
God grant me freedom from _____ *and replace it with* _____

*God, I pray for the health, prosperity, happiness and well-being of*_____
All the things I pray for myself, I pray also for _____

Review Eleventh Step Prayer on the last page of journal.

Morning Review:
(Review prayers from first page).

Plan of Eating: *Today, extra food is not an option.*

Water: ☐☐☐☐☐☐☐

Breakfast:_____
_____
_____

Lunch: _____
_____
_____

Dinner: _____
_____
_____

Snack:_____
_____
_____

Gratitudes: *(A grateful heart doesn't need to eat compulsively)*
Today, I thank God for:
_____
_____
_____
_____
_____
_____

Something I like about myself:
_____
_____
_____
_____
_____

Something to keep in mind today:
_____
_____
_____
_____

Daily Writing: Source: _____ Pages: _____

_____
_____
_____
_____
_____
_____
_____
_____
_____
_____
_____
_____
_____

Su   M   Tu   W   Th   F   Sat   Date: _____ Day #:_____

Evening Review: *(or anytime the need arises)*

Today was I:

   Resruntful?   _____

                   _____

   Selfish?   _____

                   _____

   Dishonest?   _____

                   _____

   Jealous?   _____

                   _____

   Fearful: (Of losing something? Of not getting what I want? Of being found out?)

                   _____

                   _____

   *Restless, irritable or discontented?*_____

                   _____

Was I kind and loving towards all? _____

_____

_____

*Do I owe an apology?*_____

_____

_____

What did I do for others? _____

_____

_____

*What could I have done better?*_____

_____

_____

*What did I do well?*_____

_____

_____

Freedom from Bondage: Refer to the "Self Will * God's Will" chart and the "Freedom from Bondage" reading on the last pages of this journal.

God grant me freedom from   _____ *and replace it with* _____
God grant me freedom from   _____ *and replace it with* _____
God grant me freedom from   _____ *and replace it with* _____
God grant me freedom from   _____ *and replace it with* _____

*God, I pray for the health, prosperity, happiness and well-being of*_____
All the things I pray for myself, I pray also for _____

Review Eleventh Step Prayer on the last page of journal.

Morning Review:
(Review prayers from first page).

Plan of Eating: *Today, extra food is not an option.*

Water: ☐☐☐☐☐☐☐

Breakfast:_____
_____
_____

Lunch: _____
_____
_____

Dinner: _____
_____
_____

Snack:_____
_____
_____

Gratitudes: *(A grateful heart doesn't need to eat compulsively)*
Today, I thank God for:

_____
_____
_____
_____
_____
_____

Something I like about myself:

_____
_____
_____
_____
_____

Something to keep in mind today:

_____
_____
_____
_____
_____

Daily Writing: Source: _____ Pages: _____

_____
_____
_____
_____
_____
_____
_____
_____
_____
_____
_____
_____
_____
_____
_____

Su   M   Tu   W   Th   F   Sat   Date: _____ Day #:_____

Evening Review: *(or anytime the need arises)*

Today was I:

   Resentful? _____

                    _____

   Selfish? _____

                    _____

   Dishonest? _____

                    _____

   Jealous? _____

                    _____

   Fearful: (Of losing something? Of not getting what I want? Of being found out?)

                    _____

                    _____

   *Restless, irritable or discontented?*_____

                    _____

Was I kind and loving towards all? _____

_____

*Do I owe an apology?*_____

_____

What did I do for others? _____

_____

*What could I have done better?*_____

_____

*What did I do well?*_____

_____

_____

Freedom from Bondage: Refer to the "Self Will * God's Will" chart and the "Freedom from Bondage" reading on the last pages of this journal.

God grant me freedom from _____ *and replace it with* _____
God grant me freedom from _____ *and replace it with* _____
God grant me freedom from _____ *and replace it with* _____
God grant me freedom from _____ *and replace it with* _____

*God, I pray for the health, prosperity, happiness and well-being of*_____
All the things I pray for myself, I pray also for _____

Review Eleventh Step Prayer on the last page of journal.

Morning Review:
(Review prayers from first page).

Plan of Eating: *Today, extra food is not an option.*

Water: ☐☐☐☐☐☐☐

Breakfast:_____
_____
_____

Lunch: _____
_____
_____

Dinner: _____
_____
_____

Snack:_____
_____
_____

Gratitudes: *(A grateful heart doesn't need to eat compulsively)*
Today, I thank God for:
_____
_____
_____
_____
_____
_____

Something I like about myself:
_____
_____
_____
_____
_____

Something to keep in mind today:
_____
_____
_____

Daily Writing: Source: _____ Pages: _____

_____
_____
_____
_____
_____
_____
_____
_____
_____
_____
_____
_____
_____
_____
_____

Su   M   Tu   W   Th   F   Sat   Date: _____ Day #:_____

Evening Review: *(or anytime the need arises)*

Today was I:

Resentful?   _____

          _____

Selfish?   _____

          _____

Dishonest?   _____

          _____

Jealous?   _____

          _____

Fearful: (Of losing something? Of not getting what I want? Of being found out?)

          _____

          _____

Restless, irritable or discontented?_____

          _____

Was I kind and loving towards all? _____

_____

_____

Do I owe an apology?_____

_____

_____

What did I do for others? _____

_____

_____

What could I have done better?_____

_____

_____

What did I do well?_____

_____

_____

Freedom from Bondage: Refer to the "Self Will * God's Will" chart and the "Freedom from Bondage" reading on the last pages of this journal.

God grant me freedom from   _____ *and replace it with* _____
God grant me freedom from   _____ *and replace it with* _____
God grant me freedom from   _____ *and replace it with* _____
God grant me freedom from   _____ *and replace it with* _____

*God, I pray for the health, prosperity, happiness and well-being of*_____
All the things I pray for myself, I pray also for _____

Review Eleventh Step Prayer on the last page of journal.

Morning Review:
(Review prayers from first page).

Plan of Eating: *Today, extra food is not an option.*

Water: ⬜⬜⬜⬜⬜⬜⬜

Breakfast:_____
_____
_____

Lunch: _____
_____
_____

Dinner: _____
_____
_____

Snack:_____
_____
_____

Gratitudes: *(A grateful heart doesn't need to eat compulsively)* *Today, I thank God for:*

_____
_____
_____
_____
_____
_____

Something I like about myself:

_____
_____
_____
_____
_____

Something to keep in mind today:

_____
_____
_____
_____
_____

Daily Writing: Source: _____ Pages: _____
_____
_____
_____
_____
_____
_____
_____
_____
_____
_____
_____
_____
_____
_____

Date: _____ Day #:_____

Evening Review: *(or anytime the need arises)*

Today was I:

Resentful? _____

_____

Selfish? _____

_____

Dishonest? _____

_____

Jealous? _____

_____

Fearful: (Of losing something? Of not getting what I want? Of being found out?)

_____

_____

*Restless, irritable or discontented?*_____

_____

Was I kind and loving towards all? _____

_____

_____

*Do I owe an apology?*_____

_____

_____

What did I do for others? _____

_____

_____

*What could I have done better?*_____

_____

_____

*What did I do well?*_____

_____

_____

Freedom from Bondage: Refer to the "Self Will * God's Will" chart and the "Freedom from Bondage" reading on the last pages of this journal.

God grant me freedom from _____ *and replace it with* _____
God grant me freedom from _____ *and replace it with* _____
God grant me freedom from _____ *and replace it with* _____
God grant me freedom from _____ *and replace it with* _____

*God, I pray for the health, prosperity, happiness and well-being of*_____
All the things I pray for myself, I pray also for _____

Review Eleventh Step Prayer on the last page of journal.

Morning Review:

(Review prayers from first page).

Plan of Eating: *Today, extra food is not an option.*

Water: ⬜⬜⬜⬜⬜⬜⬜

Breakfast:_____
_____
_____

Lunch: _____
_____
_____

Dinner:_____
_____
_____

Snack:_____
_____
_____

Gratitudes: *(A grateful heart doesn't need to eat compulsively)* *Today, I thank God for:*

_____
_____
_____
_____
_____
_____

Something I like about myself:

_____
_____
_____
_____

Something to keep in mind today:

_____
_____
_____
_____

Daily Writing: Source: _____ Pages: _____

_____
_____
_____
_____
_____
_____
_____
_____
_____
_____
_____
_____
_____
_____
_____

Su   M   Tu   W   Th   F   Sat   Date: _____ Day #:_____

Evening Review: *(or anytime the need arises)*

Today was I:

   Resentful? _____

   _____

   Selfish? _____

   _____

   Dishonest? _____

   _____

   Jealous? _____

   _____

   Fearful: (Of losing something? Of not getting what I want? Of being found out?)

   _____

   _____

   *Restless, irritable or discontented?*_____

_____

Was I kind and loving towards all? _____

_____

_____

*Do I owe an apology?*_____

_____

_____

What did I do for others? _____

_____

_____

*What could I have done better?*_____

_____

_____

*What did I do well?*_____

_____

_____

Freedom from Bondage: Refer to the "Self Will * God's Will" chart and the "Freedom from Bondage" reading on the last pages of this journal.

God grant me freedom from _____ *and replace it with* _____

God grant me freedom from _____ *and replace it with* _____

God grant me freedom from _____ *and replace it with* _____

God grant me freedom from _____ *and replace it with* _____

*God, I pray for the health, prosperity, happiness and well-being of*_____

All the things I pray for myself, I pray also for _____

Review Eleventh Step Prayer on the last page of journal.

Morning Review:

(Review prayers from first page).

Plan of Eating: *Today, extra food is not an option.*

Water: ☐☐☐☐☐☐☐☐

Breakfast:_____

_____

_____

Lunch: _____

_____

_____

Dinner: _____

_____

_____

Snack:_____

_____

_____

Gratitudes: *(A grateful heart doesn't need to eat compulsively)* *Today, I thank God for:*

_____

_____

_____

_____

_____

_____

Something I like about myself:

_____

_____

_____

_____

_____

Something to keep in mind today:

_____

_____

_____

_____

_____

Daily Writing: Source: _____ Pages: _____

_____

_____

_____

_____

_____

_____

_____

_____

_____

_____

_____

_____

_____

Su   M   Tu   W   Th   F   Sat   Date: _____   Day #:_____

Evening Review: *(or anytime the need arises)*

Today was I:

  Resentful?   _____

                       _____

  Selfish?   _____

                       _____

  Dishonest?   _____

                       _____

  Jealous?   _____

                       _____

  Fearful: (Of losing something? Of not getting what I want? Of being found out?)

                       _____

                       _____

  Restless, irritable or discontented?_____

                       _____

Was I kind and loving towards all? _____

_____

_____

Do I owe an apology?_____

_____

What did I do for others? _____

_____

What could I have done better?_____

_____

_____

What did I do well?_____

_____

_____

Freedom from Bondage: Refer to the "Self Will * God's Will" chart and the "Freedom from Bondage" reading on the last pages of this journal.

God grant me freedom from _____ *and replace it with* _____
God grant me freedom from _____ *and replace it with* _____
God grant me freedom from _____ *and replace it with* _____
God grant me freedom from _____ *and replace it with* _____

God, I pray for the health, prosperity, happiness and well-being of_____
All the things I pray for myself, I pray also for _____

Review Eleventh Step Prayer on the last page of journal.

Morning Review:
(*Review prayers from first page*).

Plan of Eating: *Today, extra food is not an option.*

Water: ☐☐☐☐☐☐☐

Breakfast:_____
_____
_____

Lunch: _____
_____
_____

Dinner: _____
_____
_____

Snack:_____
_____
_____

Gratitudes: (*A grateful heart doesn't need to eat compulsively*) Today, I thank God for:

_____
_____
_____
_____
_____
_____

Something I like about myself:

_____
_____
_____
_____
_____

Something to keep in mind today:

_____
_____
_____
_____
_____

Daily Writing: Source: _____ Pages: _____
_____
_____
_____
_____
_____
_____
_____
_____
_____
_____
_____
_____
_____
_____

Su   M   Tu   W   Th   F   Sat   Date: _____ Day #:_____

Evening Review: *(or anytime the need arises)*

Today was I:

   Resentful?   _____

                        _____

   Selfish?   _____

                        _____

   Dishonest?   _____

                        _____

   Jealous?   _____

                        _____

   Fearful: (Of losing something? Of not getting what I want? Of being found out?)

                        _____

                        _____

   *Restless, irritable or discontented?*_____

                        _____

Was I kind and loving towards all? _____

_____

_____

*Do I owe an apology?*_____

_____

_____

What did I do for others? _____

_____

_____

*What could I have done better?*_____

_____

_____

*What did I do well?*_____

_____

_____

Freedom from Bondage: Refer to the "Self Will * God's Will" chart and the "Freedom from Bondage" reading on the last pages of this journal.

God grant me freedom from _____ *and replace it with* _____
God grant me freedom from _____ *and replace it with* _____
God grant me freedom from _____ *and replace it with* _____
God grant me freedom from _____ *and replace it with* _____

*God, I pray for the health, prosperity, happiness and well-being of*_____
All the things I pray for myself, I pray also for _____

Review Eleventh Step Prayer on the last page of journal.

Morning Review:

(Review prayers from first page).

Plan of Eating: *Today, extra food is not an option.*

Water: ☐☐☐☐☐☐☐

Breakfast:_____
_____
_____

Lunch: _____
_____
_____

Dinner: _____
_____
_____

Snack:_____
_____
_____

Gratitudes: *(A grateful heart doesn't need to eat compulsively)* *Today, I thank God for:*

_____
_____
_____
_____
_____
_____

Something I like about myself:

_____
_____
_____
_____
_____

Something to keep in mind today:

_____
_____
_____
_____
_____

Daily Writing:　　　Source: _____ Pages: _____

_____
_____
_____
_____
_____
_____
_____
_____
_____
_____
_____
_____
_____
_____
_____

Evening Review: *(or anytime the need arises)*

Today was I:

  Resentful?   _____

                       _____

  Selfish?   _____

                       _____

  Dishonest?   _____

                       _____

  Jealous?   _____

                       _____

  Fearful: (Of losing something? Of not getting what I want? Of being found out?)

                       _____

                       _____

  Restless, irritable or discontented?_____

                       _____

Was I kind and loving towards all? _____

_____

Do I owe an apology?_____

_____

What did I do for others? _____

_____

What could I have done better?_____

_____

What did I do well?_____

_____

_____

Freedom from Bondage: Refer to the "Self Will * God's Will" chart and the "Freedom from Bondage" reading on the last pages of this journal.

God grant me freedom from _____ *and replace it with* _____
God grant me freedom from _____ *and replace it with* _____
God grant me freedom from _____ *and replace it with* _____
God grant me freedom from _____ *and replace it with* _____

God, I pray for the health, prosperity, happiness and well-being of_____
All the things I pray for myself, I pray also for _____

Review Eleventh Step Prayer on the last page of journal.

Morning Review:
(Review prayers from first page).

Plan of Eating: *Today, extra food is not an option.*

Water: ▢▢▢▢▢▢▢

Breakfast:_____
_____
_____

Lunch: _____
_____
_____

Dinner: _____
_____
_____

Snack:_____
_____
_____

Gratitudes: *(A grateful heart doesn't need to eat compulsively)*
Today, I thank God for:
_____
_____
_____
_____
_____
_____

Something I like about myself:
_____
_____
_____
_____
_____

Something to keep in mind today:
_____
_____
_____
_____
_____

Daily Writing: Source: _____ Pages: _____

_____
_____
_____
_____
_____
_____
_____
_____
_____
_____
_____
_____
_____
_____
_____
_____

Su M Tu W Th F Sat   Date: _____ Day #:_____

Evening Review: *(or anytime the need arises)*

Today was I:

   Resentful? _____

_____

   Selfish? _____

_____

   Dishonest? _____

_____

   Jealous? _____

_____

   Fearful: (Of losing something? Of not getting what I want? Of being found out?)

_____

_____

   *Restless, irritable or discontented?*_____

_____

Was I kind and loving towards all? _____

_____

_____

Do I owe an apology? _____

_____

_____

What did I do for others? _____

_____

_____

*What could I have done better?*_____

_____

_____

*What did I do well?*_____

_____

_____

Freedom from Bondage: Refer to the "Self Will * God's Will" chart and the "Freedom from Bondage" reading on the last pages of this journal.

God grant me freedom from _____ *and replace it with*_____
God grant me freedom from _____ *and replace it with*_____
God grant me freedom from _____ *and replace it with*_____
God grant me freedom from _____ *and replace it with*_____

*God, I pray for the health, prosperity, happiness and well-being of*_____
All the things I pray for myself, I pray also for _____

Review Eleventh Step Prayer on the last page of journal.

Morning Review:
(*Review prayers from first page*).

Plan of Eating: *Today, extra food is not an option.*

Water: ☐☐☐☐☐☐☐

Breakfast:_____
_____
_____

Lunch: _____
_____
_____

Dinner: _____
_____
_____

Snack:_____
_____
_____

Gratitudes: (*A grateful heart doesn't need to eat compulsively*)
Today, I thank God for:
_____
_____
_____
_____
_____
_____

Something I like about myself:
_____
_____
_____
_____
_____

Something to keep in mind today:
_____
_____
_____
_____

Daily Writing: Source: _____ Pages: _____

_____
_____
_____
_____
_____
_____
_____
_____
_____
_____
_____
_____
_____
_____

Su   M   Tu   W   Th   F   Sat   Date: _____ Day #:_____

Evening Review: *(or anytime the need arises)*

Today was I:

   Resentful? _____

   _____

   Selfish? _____

   _____

   Dishonest? _____

   _____

   Jealous? _____

   _____

   Fearful: (Of losing something? Of not getting what I want? Of being found out?)

   _____

   _____

   *Restless, irritable or discontented?*_____

   _____

Was I kind and loving towards all? _____

_____

_____

*Do I owe an apology?*_____

_____

_____

What did I do for others? _____

_____

_____

*What could I have done better?*_____

_____

_____

*What did I do well?*_____

_____

_____

Freedom from Bondage: Refer to the "Self Will * God's Will" chart and the "Freedom from Bondage" reading on the last pages of this journal.

God grant me freedom from _____ *and replace it with* _____
God grant me freedom from _____ *and replace it with* _____
God grant me freedom from _____ *and replace it with* _____
God grant me freedom from _____ *and replace it with* _____

*God, I pray for the health, prosperity, happiness and well-being of*_____
All the things I pray for myself, I pray also for _____

Review Eleventh Step Prayer on the last page of journal.

Morning Review:
(*Review prayers from first page*).

Plan of Eating: *Today, extra food is not an option.*

Water: ☐☐☐☐☐☐☐☐

Breakfast:_____
_____
_____

Lunch: _____
_____
_____

Dinner: _____
_____
_____

Snack:_____
_____
_____

Gratitudes: (*A grateful heart doesn't need to eat compulsively*)
Today, I thank God for:
_____
_____
_____
_____
_____
_____

Something I like about myself:
_____
_____
_____
_____
_____

Something to keep in mind today:
_____
_____
_____
_____

Daily Writing: Source: _____ Pages: _____
_____
_____
_____
_____
_____
_____
_____
_____
_____
_____
_____
_____
_____

Su   M   Tu   W   Th   F   Sat   Date: _____ Day #:_____

Evening Review: *(or anytime the need arises)*

Today was I:

   Resentful? _____

                           _____

   Selfish? _____

                           _____

   Dishonest? _____

                           _____

   Jealous? _____

   Fearful: (Of losing something? Of not getting what I want? Of being found out?)

                           _____

                           _____

   Restless, irritable or discontented? _____

                           _____

Was I kind and loving towards all? _____

_____

_____

Do I owe an apology? _____

_____

_____

What did I do for others? _____

_____

_____

What could I have done better? _____

_____

_____

What did I do well? _____

_____

_____

Freedom from Bondage: Refer to the "Self Will * God's Will" chart and the "Freedom from Bondage" reading on the last pages of this journal.

God grant me freedom from _____ *and replace it with* _____
God grant me freedom from _____ *and replace it with* _____
God grant me freedom from _____ *and replace it with* _____
God grant me freedom from _____ *and replace it with* _____

God, I pray for the health, prosperity, happiness and well-being of _____
All the things I pray for myself, I pray also for _____

Review Eleventh Step Prayer on the last page of journal.

Morning Review:
(Review prayers from first page).

Plan of Eating: *Today, extra food is not an option.*

Water: ☐☐☐☐☐☐☐

Breakfast:_____
_____
_____

Lunch: _____
_____
_____

Dinner: _____
_____
_____

Snack:_____
_____
_____

Gratitudes: *(A grateful heart doesn't need to eat compulsively)* *Today, I thank God for:*
_____
_____
_____
_____
_____
_____

Something I like about myself:
_____
_____
_____
_____
_____

Something to keep in mind today:
_____
_____
_____
_____
_____

Daily Writing: Source: _____ Pages: _____
_____
_____
_____
_____
_____
_____
_____
_____
_____
_____
_____
_____
_____
_____

Su   M   Tu   W   Th   F   Sat   Date: _____ Day #:_____

Evening Review: *(or anytime the need arises)*

Today was I:

  Resentful? _____

  _____

  Selfish? _____

  _____

  Dishonest? _____

  _____

  Jealous? _____

  _____

  Fearful: (Of losing something? Of not getting what I want? Of being found out?)

  _____

  _____

  *Restless, irritable or discontented?*_____

  _____

Was I kind and loving towards all? _____

_____

_____

*Do I owe an apology?*_____

_____

_____

What did I do for others? _____

_____

_____

*What could I have done better?*_____

_____

_____

*What did I do well?*_____

_____

_____

Freedom from Bondage: Refer to the "Self Will * God's Will" chart and the "Freedom from Bondage" reading on the last pages of this journal.

God grant me freedom from _____ *and replace it with* _____
God grant me freedom from _____ *and replace it with* _____
God grant me freedom from _____ *and replace it with* _____
God grant me freedom from _____ *and replace it with* _____

*God, I pray for the health, prosperity, happiness and well-being of*_____
All the things I pray for myself, I pray also for _____

Review Eleventh Step Prayer on the last page of journal.

Morning Review:
(*Review prayers from first page*).

Plan of Eating: *Today, extra food is not an option.*

Water: ☐☐☐☐☐☐☐☐

Breakfast:_____
_____
_____

Lunch: _____
_____
_____

Dinner: _____
_____
_____

Snack:_____
_____
_____

Gratitudes: (*A grateful heart doesn't need to eat compulsively*) Today, I thank God for:

_____
_____
_____
_____
_____
_____

Something I like about myself:

_____
_____
_____
_____
_____

Something to keep in mind today:

_____
_____
_____
_____
_____

Daily Writing:　　　Source: _____ Pages: _____

_____
_____
_____
_____
_____
_____
_____
_____
_____
_____
_____
_____
_____
_____

Evening Review: *(or anytime the need arises)*

Today was I:

   Resentful?   _____

                      _____

   Selfish?   _____

                      _____

   Dishonest?   _____

                      _____

   Jealous?   _____

                      _____

   Fearful: (Of losing something? Of not getting what I want? Of being found out?)

                      _____

                      _____

   *Restless, irritable or discontented?*_____

                      _____

Was I kind and loving towards all? _____

_____

*Do I owe an apology?*_____

_____

_____

What did I do for others? _____

_____

_____

*What could I have done better?*_____

_____

_____

*What did I do well?*_____

_____

_____

Freedom from Bondage: Refer to the "Self Will * God's Will" chart and the "Freedom from Bondage" reading on the last pages of this journal.

God grant me freedom from _____ *and replace it with* _____
God grant me freedom from _____ *and replace it with* _____
God grant me freedom from _____ *and replace it with* _____
God grant me freedom from _____ *and replace it with* _____

*God, I pray for the health, prosperity, happiness and well-being of*_____
All the things I pray for myself, I pray also for _____

Review Eleventh Step Prayer on the last page of journal.

Morning Review:
(Review prayers from first page).

Plan of Eating: *Today, extra food is not an option.*

Water: ☐☐☐☐☐☐☐

Breakfast:_____
_____
_____

Lunch: _____
_____
_____

Dinner: _____
_____
_____

Snack:_____
_____
_____

Gratitudes: *(A grateful heart doesn't need to eat compulsively)*
Today, I thank God for:
_____
_____
_____
_____
_____

Something I like about myself:
_____
_____
_____
_____

Something to keep in mind today:
_____
_____
_____

Daily Writing: Source: _____ Pages: _____

_____
_____
_____
_____
_____
_____
_____
_____
_____
_____
_____
_____
_____
_____
_____

Su   M   Tu   W   Th   F   Sat   Date: _____ Day #:_____

Evening Review: *(or anytime the need arises)*

Today was I:

  Resentful?   _____

                       _____

  Selfish?   _____

                       _____

  Dishonest?   _____

                       _____

  Jealous?   _____

                       _____

  Fearful: (Of losing something? Of not getting what I want? Of being found out?)

                       _____

                       _____

  *Restless, irritable or discontented?*_____

                       _____

Was I kind and loving towards all? _____

_____

*Do I owe an apology?*_____

_____

What did I do for others? _____

_____

*What could I have done better?*_____

_____

_____

*What did I do well?*_____

_____

_____

Freedom from Bondage: Refer to the "Self Will * God's Will" chart and the "Freedom from Bondage" reading on the last pages of this journal.

God grant me freedom from _____ *and replace it with* _____
God grant me freedom from _____ *and replace it with* _____
God grant me freedom from _____ *and replace it with* _____
God grant me freedom from _____ *and replace it with* _____

*God, I pray for the health, prosperity, happiness and well-being of*_____
All the things I pray for myself, I pray also for _____

Review Eleventh Step Prayer on the last page of journal.

Morning Review:

(*Review prayers from first page*).

Plan of Eating: *Today, extra food is not an option.*

Water: ☐☐☐☐☐☐☐

Breakfast:_____

_____

_____

Lunch: _____

_____

_____

Dinner: _____

_____

_____

Snack:_____

_____

_____

Gratitudes: (*A grateful heart doesn't need to eat compulsively*) *Today, I thank God for:*

_____

_____

_____

_____

_____

Something I like about myself:

_____

_____

_____

_____

_____

Something to keep in mind today:

_____

_____

_____

_____

Daily Writing: Source: _____ Pages: _____

_____

_____

_____

_____

_____

_____

_____

_____

_____

_____

_____

_____

_____

_____

Su   M   Tu   W   Th   F   Sat   Date: _____   Day #:_____

Evening Review: *(or anytime the need arises)*

Today was I:

Resentful?   _____

_____

Selfish?   _____

_____

Dishonest?   _____

_____

Jealous?   _____

_____

Fearful: (Of losing something? Of not getting what I want? Of being found out?)

_____

_____

*Restless, irritable or discontented?*_____

_____

Was I kind and loving towards all? _____

_____

Do I owe an apology? _____

_____

_____

What did I do for others? _____

_____

_____

*What could I have done better?*_____

_____

_____

*What did I do well?*_____

_____

_____

Freedom from Bondage: Refer to the "Self Will * God's Will" chart and the "Freedom from Bondage" reading on the last pages of this journal.

God grant me freedom from _____ *and replace it with* _____
God grant me freedom from _____ *and replace it with* _____
God grant me freedom from _____ *and replace it with* _____
God grant me freedom from _____ *and replace it with* _____

*God, I pray for the health, prosperity, happiness and well-being of*_____
All the things I pray for myself, I pray also for _____

Review Eleventh Step Prayer on the last page of journal.

Morning Review:
(Review prayers from first page).

Plan of Eating: *Today, extra food is not an option.*

Water: ☐ ☐ ☐ ☐ ☐ ☐ ☐

Breakfast:_____
_____
_____

Lunch: _____
_____
_____

Dinner: _____
_____
_____

Snack:_____
_____
_____

Gratitudes: *(A grateful heart doesn't need to eat compulsively)*
Today, I thank God for:

_____
_____
_____
_____
_____
_____

Something I like about myself:

_____
_____
_____
_____
_____

Something to keep in mind today:

_____
_____
_____
_____
_____

Daily Writing: Source: _____ Pages: _____

_____
_____
_____
_____
_____
_____
_____
_____
_____
_____
_____
_____
_____
_____

Su   M   Tu   W   Th   F   Sat   Date: _____ Day #:_____

Evening Review: *(or anytime the need arises)*

Today was I:

   Resentful? _____

   _____

   Selfish? _____

   _____

   Dishonest? _____

   _____

   Jealous? _____

   _____

   Fearful: (Of losing something? Of not getting what I want? Of being found out?)

   _____

   _____

   Restless, irritable or discontented?_____

   _____

Was I kind and loving towards all? _____

_____

_____

Do I owe an apology?_____

_____

_____

What did I do for others? _____

_____

_____

What could I have done better?_____

_____

_____

What did I do well?_____

_____

_____

Freedom from Bondage: Refer to the "Self Will * God's Will" chart and the "Freedom from Bondage" reading on the last pages of this journal.

God grant me freedom from _____ *and replace it with* _____
God grant me freedom from _____ *and replace it with* _____
God grant me freedom from _____ *and replace it with* _____
God grant me freedom from _____ *and replace it with* _____

God, I pray for the health, prosperity, happiness and well-being of_____
All the things I pray for myself, I pray also for _____

Review Eleventh Step Prayer on the last page of journal.

Morning Review:
(*Review prayers from first page*).

Plan of Eating: *Today, extra food is not an option.*

Water: ☐☐☐☐☐☐☐

Breakfast:_____
_____
_____

Lunch: _____
_____
_____

Dinner: _____
_____
_____

Snack:_____
_____
_____

Gratitudes: (*A grateful heart doesn't need to eat compulsively*) *Today, I thank God for:*

_____
_____
_____
_____
_____
_____

Something I like about myself:

_____
_____
_____
_____
_____

Something to keep in mind today:

_____
_____
_____
_____
_____

Daily Writing: Source: _____ Pages: _____

_____
_____
_____
_____
_____
_____
_____
_____
_____
_____
_____
_____
_____
_____

Su M Tu W Th F Sat   Date: _____ Day #:_____

Evening Review: *(or anytime the need arises)*

Today was I:

Resentful?   _____

_____

Selfish?   _____

_____

Dishonest?   _____

_____

Jealous?   _____

_____

Fearful: (Of losing something? Of not getting what I want? Of being found out?)

_____

_____

Restless, irritable or discontented?_____

_____

Was I kind and loving towards all? _____

_____

*Do I owe an apology?*_____

_____

What did I do for others? _____

_____

*What could I have done better?*_____

_____

*What did I do well?*_____

_____

_____

Freedom from Bondage: Refer to the "Self Will * God's Will" chart and the "Freedom from Bondage" reading on the last pages of this journal.

God grant me freedom from _____ *and replace it with* _____

God grant me freedom from _____ *and replace it with* _____

God grant me freedom from _____ *and replace it with* _____

God grant me freedom from _____ *and replace it with* _____

*God, I pray for the health, prosperity, happiness and well-being of*_____

All the things I pray for myself, I pray also for _____

Review Eleventh Step Prayer on the last page of journal.

Morning Review:
(Review prayers from first page).

Plan of Eating: *Today, extra food is not an option.*

Water: ☐☐☐☐☐☐☐

Breakfast:_____
_____
_____

Lunch: _____
_____
_____

Dinner: _____
_____
_____

Snack:_____
_____
_____

Gratitudes: *(A grateful heart doesn't need to eat compulsively)* *Today, I thank God for:*
_____
_____
_____
_____
_____
_____

Something I like about myself:
_____
_____
_____
_____
_____

Something to keep in mind today:
_____
_____
_____
_____

Daily Writing: Source: _____ Pages: _____

_____
_____
_____
_____
_____
_____
_____
_____
_____
_____
_____
_____
_____
_____
_____

Su   M   Tu   W   Th   F   Sat   Date: _____ Day #:_____

Evening Review: *(or anytime the need arises)*

Today was I:

   Resentful? _____

_____

   Selfish? _____

_____

   Dishonest? _____

_____

   Jealous? _____

_____

   Fearful: (Of losing something? Of not getting what I want? Of being found out?)

_____

_____

   Restless, irritable or discontented? _____

_____

Was I kind and loving towards all? _____

_____

_____

Do I owe an apology? _____

_____

_____

What did I do for others? _____

_____

_____

What could I have done better? _____

_____

_____

What did I do well? _____

_____

_____

Freedom from Bondage: Refer to the "Self Will * God's Will" chart and the "Freedom from Bondage" reading on the last pages of this journal.

God grant me freedom from _____ *and replace it with* _____
God grant me freedom from _____ *and replace it with* _____
God grant me freedom from _____ *and replace it with* _____
God grant me freedom from _____ *and replace it with* _____

God, I pray for the health, prosperity, happiness and well-being of _____
All the things I pray for myself, I pray also for _____

Review Eleventh Step Prayer on the last page of journal.

Morning Review:
(*Review prayers from first page*).

Plan of Eating: *Today, extra food is not an option.*

Water: ☐☐☐☐☐☐☐

Breakfast:_____
_____
_____

Lunch: _____
_____
_____

Dinner:_____
_____
_____

Snack:_____
_____
_____

Gratitudes: (*A grateful heart doesn't need to eat compulsively*)
Today, I thank God for:

_____
_____
_____
_____
_____
_____

Something I like about myself:

_____
_____
_____
_____
_____

Something to keep in mind today:

_____
_____
_____
_____

Daily Writing: Source: _____ Pages: _____

_____
_____
_____
_____
_____
_____
_____
_____
_____
_____
_____
_____
_____
_____

Su   M   Tu   W   Th   F   Sat   Date: _____ Day #: _____

Evening Review: *(or anytime the need arises)*

Today was I:

    Resentful? _____

    _____

    Selfish? _____

    _____

    Dishonest? _____

    _____

    Jealous? _____

    _____

    Fearful: (Of losing something? Of not getting what I want? Of being found out?)

    _____

    _____

    *Restless, irritable or discontented?*_____

    _____

Was I kind and loving towards all? _____

_____

*Do I owe an apology?*_____

_____

_____

What did I do for others? _____

_____

_____

*What could I have done better?*_____

_____

_____

*What did I do well?*_____

_____

_____

Freedom from Bondage: Refer to the "Self Will * God's Will" chart and the "Freedom from Bondage" reading on the last pages of this journal.

God grant me freedom from _____ *and replace it with* _____
God grant me freedom from _____ *and replace it with* _____
God grant me freedom from _____ *and replace it with* _____
God grant me freedom from _____ *and replace it with* _____

*God, I pray for the health, prosperity, happiness and well-being of*_____
All the things I pray for myself, I pray also for _____

Review Eleventh Step Prayer on the last page of journal.

Morning Review:

(Review prayers from first page).

Plan of Eating: *Today, extra food is not an option.*

Water: ☐☐☐☐☐☐☐

Breakfast:_____
_____
_____

Lunch: _____
_____
_____

Dinner: _____
_____
_____

Snack:_____
_____
_____

Gratitudes: *(A grateful heart doesn't need to eat compulsively)* *Today, I thank God for:*

_____
_____
_____
_____
_____
_____

Something I like about myself:

_____
_____
_____
_____
_____

Something to keep in mind today:

_____
_____
_____
_____

Daily Writing: Source: _____ Pages: _____

_____
_____
_____
_____
_____
_____
_____
_____
_____
_____
_____
_____
_____
_____

Su   M   Tu   W   Th   F   Sat   Date: _____ Day #:_____

Evening Review: *(or anytime the need arises)*

Today was I:

    Resentful? _____

    _____

    Selfish? _____

    _____

    Dishonest? _____

    _____

    Jealous? _____

    _____

    Fearful: (Of losing something? Of not getting what I want? Of being found out?)

    _____

    _____

    *Restless, irritable or discontented?*_____

    _____

Was I kind and loving towards all? _____

_____

*Do I owe an apology?*_____

_____

What did I do for others? _____

_____

*What could I have done better?*_____

_____

_____

*What did I do well?*_____

_____

_____

Freedom from Bondage: Refer to the "Self Will * God's Will" chart and the "Freedom from Bondage" reading on the last pages of this journal.

God grant me freedom from _____ *and replace it with* _____
God grant me freedom from _____ *and replace it with* _____
God grant me freedom from _____ *and replace it with* _____
God grant me freedom from _____ *and replace it with* _____

*God, I pray for the health, prosperity, happiness and well-being of*_____
All the things I pray for myself, I pray also for _____

Review Eleventh Step Prayer on the last page of journal.

Morning Review:
(Review prayers from first page).

Plan of Eating: *Today, extra food is not an option.*

Water: ☐☐☐☐☐☐☐

Breakfast:_____
_____
_____

Lunch: _____
_____
_____

Dinner: _____
_____
_____

Snack:_____
_____
_____

Gratitudes: *(A grateful heart doesn't need to eat compulsively)*
Today, I thank God for:
_____
_____
_____
_____
_____
_____

Something I like about myself:
_____
_____
_____
_____
_____

Something to keep in mind today:
_____
_____
_____
_____
_____

Daily Writing: Source: _____ Pages: _____

_____
_____
_____
_____
_____
_____
_____
_____
_____
_____
_____
_____
_____
_____

Su M Tu W Th F Sat   Date: _____ Day #:_____

Evening Review: *(or anytime the need arises)*

Today was I:

   Resentful? _____

   _____

   Selfish? _____

   _____

   Dishonest? _____

   _____

   Jealous? _____

   _____

   Fearful: (Of losing something? Of not getting what I want? Of being found out?)

   _____

   _____

   *Restless, irritable or discontented?*_____

   _____

Was I kind and loving towards all? _____

_____

_____

Do I owe an apology? _____

_____

_____

What did I do for others? _____

_____

_____

*What could I have done better?*_____

_____

_____

*What did I do well?*_____

_____

_____

Freedom from Bondage: Refer to the "Self Will * God's Will" chart and the "Freedom from Bondage" reading on the last pages of this journal.

God grant me freedom from _____ *and replace it with* _____
God grant me freedom from _____ *and replace it with* _____
God grant me freedom from _____ *and replace it with* _____
God grant me freedom from _____ *and replace it with* _____

*God, I pray for the health, prosperity, happiness and well-being of*_____
All the things I pray for myself, I pray also for _____

Review Eleventh Step Prayer on the last page of journal.

Morning Review:

(Review prayers from first page).

Plan of Eating: *Today, extra food is not an option.*

Water: □□□□□□□

Breakfast:_____

_____

_____

Lunch: _____

_____

_____

Dinner: _____

_____

_____

Snack:_____

_____

_____

Gratitudes: *(A grateful heart doesn't need to eat compulsively)*
Today, I thank God for:

_____

_____

_____

_____

_____

_____

Something I like about myself:

_____

_____

_____

_____

_____

Something to keep in mind today:

_____

_____

_____

_____

_____

Daily Writing: Source: _____ Pages: _____

_____

_____

_____

_____

_____

_____

_____

_____

_____

_____

_____

_____

_____

_____

_____

Su   M   Tu   W   Th   F   Sat   Date: _____ Day #:_____

Evening Review: *(or anytime the need arises)*

Today was I:

   Resentful? _____

_____

   Selfish? _____

_____

   Dishonest? _____

_____

   Jealous? _____

_____

   Fearful: (Of losing something? Of not getting what I want? Of being found out?)

_____

_____

   *Restless, irritable or discontented?*_____

_____

Was I kind and loving towards all? _____

_____

_____

*Do I owe an apology?*_____

_____

_____

What did I do for others? _____

_____

_____

*What could I have done better?*_____

_____

_____

*What did I do well?*_____

_____

_____

Freedom from Bondage: Refer to the "Self Will * God's Will" chart and the "Freedom from Bondage" reading on the last pages of this journal.

God grant me freedom from _____ *and replace it with* _____
God grant me freedom from _____ *and replace it with* _____
God grant me freedom from _____ *and replace it with* _____
God grant me freedom from _____ *and replace it with* _____

*God, I pray for the health, prosperity, happiness and well-being of*_____
All the things I pray for myself, I pray also for _____

Review Eleventh Step Prayer on the last page of journal.

Daily Writing: Source: _____   Pages: _____

Daily Writing: Source:_____ Pages:_____

_____
_____
_____
_____
_____
_____
_____
_____
_____
_____
_____
_____
_____
_____
_____
_____
_____
_____
_____
_____
_____
_____
_____
_____
_____
_____
_____
_____
_____
_____
_____
_____
_____
_____

Daily Writing: Source: _____   Pages: _____

Daily Writing: Source:_____ Pages: _____

Daily Writing: Source: _____   Pages: _____

_____
_____
_____
_____
_____
_____
_____
_____
_____
_____
_____
_____
_____
_____
_____
_____
_____
_____
_____
_____
_____
_____
_____
_____
_____
_____
_____
_____
_____
_____
_____
_____
_____
_____
_____
_____
_____
_____

Daily Writing: Source:_____ Pages: _____

Daily Writing: Source: _____ Pages: _____

Daily Writing: Source:_____   Pages: _____

Daily Writing: Source: _____   Pages: _____

Daily Writing: Source:_____ Pages:_____

_____
_____
_____
_____
_____
_____
_____
_____
_____
_____
_____
_____
_____
_____
_____
_____
_____
_____
_____
_____
_____
_____
_____
_____
_____
_____
_____
_____
_____
_____
_____
_____
_____
_____
_____
_____
_____
_____
_____
_____
_____

Notes and Numbers

Excerpts from Alcoholics Anonymous literature are reprinted with the permission of Alcoholics Anonymous World Services, Inc.

Excerpts from Overeaters Anonymous literature are reprinted with the permission of Overeaters Anonymous, Inc.

SELF-WILL		GOD'S WILL
Selfishness/Self-Seeking	*	Interest in Others/Altruism
Being Self-Centered	*	Being Love-Centered/God-Centered
Dishonesty	*	Honesty
Fear	*	Faith and Trust in God
Being Inconsiderate	*	Being Considerate
Pride	*	Humility, Seeking God's Will
Greed	*	Giving and Sharing
Lustful Thoughts	*	Respectful Thoughts
Anger	*	Serenity/Acceptance
Envy	*	Gratitude
Judgement	*	Acceptance
Sloth/Procrastination	*	Taking Right Action
Gluttony	*	Moderation
Impatience	*	Patience
Intolerance	*	Tolerance
Resentment	*	Forgiveness
Hate	*	Love and Concern for Others
Harmful Acts	*	Good Deeds
Self-Pity	*	Self-Forgetfulness
Self-Justification	*	Humility and Truth
Self-Importance	*	Modesty
Self-Condemnation	*	Self-Forgiveness
Suspicion/Jealousy	*	Trust
Doubt	*	Faith

(Big Book Study, OA Region Seven)

Eleventh Step Prayer
(The Twelve Steps and Twelve Traditions of Alcoholics Anonymous, page 99)

"Lord, make me a channel of thy peace—

that where there is hatred, I may bring love—

that where there is wrong, I may bring the spirit of forgiveness—

that where there is discord, I may bring harmony—

that where there is error, I may bring truth—

that where there is doubt, I may bring faith—

that where there is despair, I may bring hope—

that where there are shadows, I may bring light—

that where there is sadness, I may bring joy.

Lord, grant that I may seek rather to comfort than to be comforted—

to understand, than to be understood—

to love, than to be loved.

For it is by self-forgetting that one finds. It is by forgiving that one is forgiven.

It is by dying that one awakens to Eternal Life. Amen."

Freedom from Bondage Prayer
(Alcoholics Anonymous, Fourth Edition, page 552)

"If you have a resentment you want to be free of, if you will pray for the person or

the thing that you resent, you will be free. If you will ask in prayer for everything

you want for yourself to be given to them, you will be free. Ask for their health,

their prosperity, their happiness, and you will be free. Even when you don't really

want it for them and your prayers are only words and you don't mean it, go ahead

and do it anyway. Do it every day for two weeks, and you will find that you have

come to mean it and to want it for them, and you will realize that where you used to

feel bitterness and resentment and hatred, you now feel compassionate

understanding and love."

Ready to order your next Region One Daily Journal?

Order through oaregion1.org/journals

(Second Edition, soft-cover 6"x9" or 8.5"x11" version)

or

Pick one up in person at our annual Region One Convention!

If you have questions about our Daily Journal please email

journals@oaregion1.org.

OVEREATERS ANONYMOUS

ALASKA · ALBERTA · N.W.
TERRITORIES · SASKATCHEWAN
YUKON · BRITISH COLUMBIA
OREGON · IDAHO
WASHINGTON
MONTANA
WYOMING

REGION ONE

Made in the USA
Las Vegas, NV
14 October 2023

79084481R00125